SLS

B48 208 673 6

D0315029

Produced by Fowke & Co. for Hodder Children's Books

Published by Hodder Children's Books 2003

0 340 85187 2

10 9 8 7 6 5 4 3

Hodder Children's Books
a division of Hodder Headline Limited
338 Euston Road
London NW1 3BH

Printed and bound in Great Britain by Bookmarque Ltd, Croydon
A Catalogue record for this book is available from the British Library

Who? What? When? World War II

By Bob Fowke
With drawings by the same

Hodder
Children's
Books

a division of Hodder Headline Limited

Plea for forgiveness

World War II was the bloodiest war the world has ever seen. For six long years, war raged over most of the surface of the earth. Between forty and sixty million people are reckoned to have died, including eleven million defenceless victims, deliberately murdered by the Nazis.

War on this scale needs a library of books to describe it and indeed a library of books has been written, and is still being written. This book takes the most important bits, the bits you need to know about for your studies or simply if you want to grasp the basics of what happened. Pity the poor author who had to decide what those important bits are, and forgive him if he's left out things or people that you think should be in.

Bob Fowke

evil
madmen

bombing
raids

spies

defenders

How to read this book

weapons

battles

fighters

Entries are listed alphabetically.
If you prefer, you can find which
page someone or something is
on by looking in the index
starting on page 123.

invasions

heroes

friends

prisoners

ships

military
leaders

Words followed by* - you can
look up what they mean in the
glossary on page 122.

Names in **bold** in the text are of
people who have their own
entry. The little number in the
margin beside them shows
which page you'll find them on.

transport

On the next page, there's a time
chart showing how major events
in the war were connected.

women

politicians

entertainers

flying objects

civilians

When?

1919: Nazi Party founded.

1923: Beer Hall Putsch, the Nazis try to seize southern Germany.

1925: SS formed.

1933: Nazis take power in Germany.

1933: First concentration camps opened.

1936: Germany and Italy sign treaty and start the 'axis powers'.

March 1938: *Anschluss* - Germans take over Austria.

September 1938: Munich Crisis.

15 March 1939: Germans invade Czechoslovakia.

28 August 1939: Russo-German treaty of friendship.

1 September 1939: Germans invade Poland.

3 September 1939: Britain and France declare war on Germany.

1940: Rationing begins in Britain.

10 May 1940: Hitler invades France.

14 May 1940: Home Guard started.

26 May - 6 June 1940: Dunkirk.

13 August - 17 September 1940: Battle of Britain.

August 1940 - May 1941: The Blitz.

March 1941: Lend Lease started.

22 June 1941: Germans invade Russia.

July 1941: Start of the seige of Leningrad.

3 December 1941: USA declares war on Japan.

7 December 1941: Japanese attack Pearl Harbor.

March 1942: First 'Thousand bomber raid', on Lübeck.

March 1942: Baedecker raids on historic English towns.

July 1942: Burma/Thailand railway started.

July 1942: First Battle of El Alamein.

12 September 1942: Germans enter Stalingrad.

23 October - 4 November 1942: Second Battle of El Alamein.

15 February 1943: Fall of Singapore.

17 May 1943: Dam Busters raid on Ruhr Valley.

February 1944: Dresden bombed.

Spring 1944: Battle of Anzio.

6 June 1944: D-Day.

13 June 1944: first V1 flying bombs fall on England.

20 July 1944: Von Stauffenberg Plot to kill Hitler.

26 August 1944: De Gaulle enters liberated Paris.

8 September 1944: First V2 flying bombs fall on England.

September 1944: Battle of Arnhem.

October 1944: Battle of Leyte off the Philippines.

December 1944: Battle of the Ardennes.

February 1945: GIs land on Iwo Jima.

12 April 1945: Roosevelt dead.

30 April 1945: Hitler dead.

8 May 1945: VE Day.

6 August 1945: A-bomb dropped on Hiroshima.

air raid shelters
safer than houses

Fancy some veg on your roof? The Anderson shelter was delivered in parts to your front door and you put it up yourself. First you dug a hole in the back garden and then you laid the shelter over it. The curved roof was made up of fourteen sheets of corrugated steel. After that you piled earth on top - and you could even grow vegetables on it! Once inside you were safe as houses - well, a lot safer.

Before war began, the British government planned for deadly destruction from German bombers - up to two million casualties were expected. They gave out free Anderson air raid shelters to 1.5 million families. The Anderson shelter was so called because it was designed by a Dr David Anderson, and the Home Secretary who organised it was also called Anderson.

Meanwhile, covered trenches were dug in parks and public squares, enough to protect a further half million people. Shelters were also built in the basements of some strong buildings. When the **Blitz** began, thousands of Londoners per night took shelter in underground stations. Underground stations were uncomfortable, but they were about as safe as you could get. One of the main problems was that they were below the main drains. There were no toilets down there because there was nowhere for them to drain into. The government also built brick street shelters, but these were unpopular because they weren't safe enough.

If you hadn't got an Anderson shelter and you didn't want to sleep in the tube, you might have a Morrison shelter, named after Herbert Morrison, Minister of Home Security. This was a metal cage which you put up in a downstairs room. Morrison shelters were extremely strong and gave protection even if a two-storey house crashed down on top.

The Germans were even better prepared. They built huge public shelters in Berlin. The largest, underneath Berlin Zoo, could protect 10,000 people at a time.

I THOUGHT THIS SHELTER WAS JUST FOR PEOPLE!

Allies, the
friends - for a while

If two or more countries agree to defend each other in time of war, they're called 'allies'. In World War II, the Allies were the group of countries which banded together to defeat Germany and Japan. The most important of the Allies were firstly Britain and France 70 (before it was conquered), then Russia after **Hitler** 90 invaded in 1940, then America after **Pearl Harbor** in 1941. The Poles, the Free French and Britain's overseas cousins such as the Australians, Canadians and New Zealanders were also Allies.

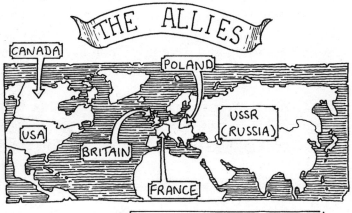

Anschluss
all Germans together

Austrians are Germans - well, almost. They speak German anyway, and their traditional costume includes leather shorts or *lederhosen* like the Germans. Before Germany became one large country, in the nineteenth century, Austri~ part, a very important part, of the German spea~ world.

70 **Hitler** wanted to unite all Germans. His first step was to unite Germany and Austria, which he did on 12 March 1938 when his army marched into Vienna, the Austrian capital. The Austrian army stood by. Hitler arrived shortly after and entered Vienna on the 14th to cheering crowds. In April the Austrians voted their agreement with the *Anschluss* which means 'Union'.

anti-aircraft guns
dodgy defensive devices

There was very little that people on the ground could do to stop bombers at the start of the war. You could
23 fly **barrage balloons**, you could man a search light or you could shoot anti-aircraft guns, 'ack-acks' as they were called in Britain.

The problem with ack-acks was that bombers were quite small things compared to the sky which is

11

extremely big. On top of that, it took an anti-aircraft shell up to fifty seconds to climb to the height of a bomber and in that time the bomber would have travelled quite a distance forward. The gunner had to aim in front if he was going to have any chance of a hit. It was so difficult that it took an average 2,000 shells per hit, which is not a very good score. Often the gunners just sent up a curtain of random shells, hoping to get lucky. The good thing about ack-ack fire was that it forced bombers to fly high, and it made people on the ground feel that someone was doing something to defend them.

In June 1944 the 'proximity fuse' was introduced. This allowed shells to go off in the general area of a bomber, near enough to damage it. When proximity fuses were combined with radar-directed searchlights, ack-acks became more effective.

Anzio, Battle of
important Italian invasion
1944

10 In 1943, the **Allies** invaded the toe of the German-occupied Italian boot from North Africa. But the Allied army were soon cooped up in Southern Italy and could not break through into the main boot. The Allied High Command decided to land an army behind the German lines and further north.

On the night of 21/22 January 1944, a combined British/American force of 50,000 men with 5,000 vehicles landed just north of the ancient town of Anzio on the west coast of Italy, fifty-nine kilometres (thirty-seven miles) south of Rome. They caught the Germans completely by surprise and the whole Allied force was on land before midnight on the 22nd. But instead of pushing quickly inland, Major-General Lucas, the Allied commander, decided to make sure of his position, thus wasting valuable time. The Germans were able to regroup and counter-attack. The Allied forces were lucky because

115 they were given secret information from **ULTRA** about the German plans. So they were at least able to

put up a good defence. But it wasn't until late spring that they were able to break free from the German stranglehold, and not until 25 May that they were able to start their victorious march inland towards Rome, which was taken on 5 June.

The Allies lost 7,000 killed and 36,000 wounded or missing in the long battle. The Germans lost 40,000 including 5,000 killed.

✗ Ardennes, Battle of
'The Battle of the Bulge'
last-ditch German fight-back
1944

The Ardennes region of Southern Belgium is not a very special place. It's a hilly wooded plateau with thin soil and a poor climate. But it's been the scene of several savage battles over the last two hundred years. The last of them, in late 1944, was also the last major German offensive of World War II.

By late 1944, victorious Allied armies were advancing deep into Germany. Germany was on its knees. **Hitler's** plan was to launch two *panzer* divisions in a lightning, last-ditch attack through the Ardennes towards the major Allied supply port of Antwerp on the Belgian coast. The attack began at 5.00 am on 16 December in cold, drizzly weather. It was a total surprise and knocked the Allied troops for six. The German infantry attacked by the light of searchlight beams reflected off low cloud in the darkness of the early hours. The poor weather meant that Allied

aircraft could do nothing to help Allied soldiers on the ground.

The Germans swept forward. By Christmas Eve they were within 6 km (4 miles) of the River Meuse - which was the furthest they got. An American force under General **Patton** moved up fast from the south and other Allied forces stormed back into action. Out of 500,000 men committed to the attack, the Germans took 100,000 casualties. They lost all their aircraft and their tanks. The **Allies** lost similar numbers, but they could afford to replace them. The Germans couldn't.

The Battle of the Ardennes is also called the 'Battle of the Bulge' because of the huge bulge which the Germans made in the Allied lines. At its largest the Bulge was 60 km (40 miles) wide and 95 km (60 miles) deep.

⚔ Arnhem, Battle of
paratroopers put in peril
September 1944

By September 1944, the Allied armies had fought their way across France to the borders of Germany. But stubborn German defences held them up. Field

81 Marshal **Montgomery** suggested a big attack in the west across the River Rhine near the Dutch town of Arnhem. This was the shortest route into the German industrial heartland of the Ruhr valley.

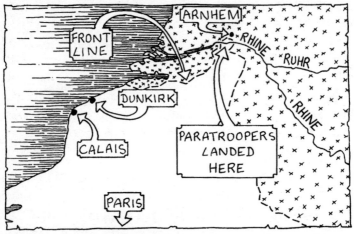

On 17 September, Allied paratroopers dropped into German occupied territory in the general area of Arnhem, to capture bridges ahead of the big Allied attack. Nearly 20,000 British paratroopers were dropped from gliders near Arnhem itself and more paratroopers were dropped in other places nearby. Unfortunately, bad weather delayed Polish paratroop reinforcements, many of the paratroopers
88 landed slap bang in the middle of two *panzer* divisions, the Germans captured an American officer carrying orders giving information about the Allied operation - and the main Allied overland attack was delayed by fierce German resistance! The British paratroopers were cut off. They fought heroically but were overwhelmed. By 25 September it was all over. More than 6,000 British and Polish paratroopers were captured, half of them wounded. The Battle of
10 Arnhem was a defeat for the **Allies**.

ARP Wardens
(Air Raid Precautions Wardens)

91
27 During the **Phoney War** and before the **Blitz** proper started, ARP wardens could be quite unpopular. Who wanted some busybody knocking on the door and telling them that there was a chink of light
26 showing through the **blackout** curtains? A load of fuss about nothing, many people thought. But once the bombs began to fall, ARP wardens became a vital part of Britain's defences. Each warden patrolled an area of about five hundred people. They patrolled on a regular basis, checking on the blackout, reporting on bombs as they fell and
8 managing the public **air raid shelter**, if there was one. Most wardens had a sandbagged headquarters post where people could come to them with problems. At the height of the Blitz it was a very dangerous job and many ARP wardens died.

✗ Atlantic, Battle of 🚢
when submarines stalked the seas
1939-43

Britain is an island. Whatever Britain needs from outside has to come either by ship or by air (at least,
70 until the Channel Tunnel was built). **Hitler** set out to cut the island off. He tried to sink as much British

17

and Allied shipping as possible and to starve Britain of vital supplies of food, metal and other materials. That way he believed that he could force Britain out of the war.

The main German weapon in this campaign was their fleet of **U-boats**. German strategy was to position a thin line of lone U-boats across the Atlantic where they waited like a long, thin fishing net. Allied merchant ships sailed in groups, known as convoys, defended by warships. Once a U-boat sighted a British convoy, it would follow it while calling to other U-boats using secret radio signals. Other U-boats would then gather round to form a 'wolf pack'. Usually they struck at night. The effect of the sudden attack in those wild, cold waters was terrifying and deadly. At the height of the battle in early 1943, 22% of all merchant ships in Allied convoys were sunk.

But the British and their allies fought back. After **Pearl Harbor** (December 1941), the USA joined the war and the tide of battle began to turn. Allied tactics against the U-boats slowly improved and the defending ships of the **Royal Navy** could now be backed up by long range air cover from air bases in

America, Iceland and Greenland as well as Britain. Meanwhile, the brain boxes at Bletchley had cracked 115 **ULTRA**. They were often able to decipher the secret German radio signals and to work out where the wolf packs were heading.

In 1943 the British began a battle of attrition*. They lured U-boats to attack despite the risks. In fact, the British were ready to accept two merchant ships lost for each U-boat lost because they knew that the Germans could no longer replace their losses fast enough. As a result, nearly a hundred U-boats were sunk in the first half of 1943. At the end of May, the German commander Grand Admiral Dönitz withdrew his wolf packs from the Atlantic - the Battle of the Atlantic was over.

atom bomb *see* **Hiroshima** *and* **Truman, Harry**

Axis Powers
friends - and enemies

In 1936 the two Fascist powers, Germany and Italy, signed a treaty of friendship, forming what became known as the 'Rome-Berlin axis' as if there was the axis of a wheel between the German and Italian capital cities. Later, the name 'Axis' came to apply to

19

all Germany's allies in World War II. The principal
Axis countries were: Germany, Italy, Japan, Romania,
Bulgaria and Hungary.

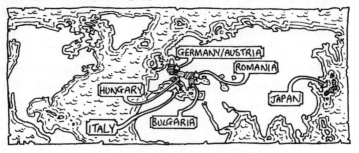

Baedeker Raids
guide book bombers

1942

On 28 March 1942, British bombers set fire to the
beautiful medieval centre of the German town of

⁶⁴ Lübeck. **Bomber Harris**, leader of British Bomber Command, ordered the raid because he wanted to prove that 'saturation bombing' could destroy an ⁷⁰ entire town. **Hitler** was so angry that he ordered a revenge bombing campaign against the most beautiful English towns. Between April and June 1942 a number of historic English towns were hit, including York, Exeter, Canterbury, Norwich and Bath. 1,637 civilians were killed.

The 'Baedeker raids' were so called after the German 'Baedeker' tourist guide book to Britain. When plans for the campaign were announced at a press conference, a German official announced that Germany would bomb every English building rated three stars in the guide.

Barbarossa, Operation
when Russia was ravaged
1941

'Barbarossa' was the German codename for their invasion of the USSR*, a vast land which covered all of what is now Russia and many other countries as well. Barbarossa was launched on 22 June 1941. In the cold, dark, early hours of the morning, 3.6 million German soldiers backed up by 3,600 tanks and 2,700 planes lurched forward into Soviet* territory. It was the largest army ever seen until that time.

The Russians fell back and the Germans swept forward on a ruthless campaign of conquest and killing. They were horrifically cruel to the Russians, who they thought of as an inferior race, and they also planned to 'cleanse' the region of its many Jews. However, autumn slowed the Germans down because the Russian roads became clogged with mud after heavy rains. The German tanks got stuck and it became very hard to bring supplies from Germany by lorry. Russian **partisans** harried the slow moving Germans. Even so, the Germans got to within thirty kilometres (eighteen miles) of the Russian capital Moscow by 31 December 1941. But that's as far as they got. The Russians began to counter-attack.

88

Joseph Stalin, the Russian leader, had built brand new industrial cities in the east of his vast country, beyond the reach of German bombers. There the Soviets churned out thousands of tanks and other weapons to replace those they had lost. Slowly but surely they forced the Germans to retreat.

The Germans lost 918,000 men killed, wounded or captured during Operation Barbarossa. It had been doomed once they failed to make a quick victory. And after it failed, they had to fight both the Russians in the East and Britain and her allies in the West.

barrage balloons
big things to bump into

Planes have to avoid bumping into things, balloons for instance, else they fall to earth. Barrage balloons were floated above likely targets and tethered to the ground by long metal cables. Enemy planes had to fly high up so as to avoid getting snarled up in the cables. High up, the planes could do less damage because they bombed less accurately. In Britain, many barrage balloons were manned by the WAAF's

(Women's Auxiliary Air Force) of 'Balloon Command'. They destroyed 231 V-1 **flying bombs** towards the end of the war.

Bismarck
that blasted battleship!

SAY! DO YOU THINK THAT'S THE BISMARCK?

The *Bismarck* was one of the most powerful battleships in the German fleet. 42,000 tons of hard steel crowned by eight massive guns and lots of smaller ones. All wasted - in the beginning at any rate. Launched in 1939, *Bismarck* spent the first two years of the war holed up in the Baltic Sea because of the blockade by the **Royal Navy**. At last, on 20 May 1941, she broke for the open seas but was spotted along with the German heavy cruiser *Scharnhorst* as she slipped past the Norwegian coast into the Atlantic Ocean. The British battleship *Prince of Wales* and the battle cruiser *Hood* raced to cut her off. Hood was sunk after a shell from the *Bismarck* struck her main magazine, causing a massive explosion. *Bismarck* escaped.

It was like having a wild, rampaging tiger free of its cage. *Bismarck* was hunted across the high seas. On 26 May her steering gear was destroyed by a torpedo launched from a flying boat. Royal Navy ships closed for the kill. She was pounded by the British battleships *King George V* and *Rodney*, and, on the morning of the 27th May, torpedoes from the British cruiser *Dorsetshire* finished her off. The *Bismarck* went down with nearly all her crew of 2,222. Just 115 were fished from the cold waters by the British sailors. The rest died.

⊘ black market
where to go for those little extras

The black market was not where you went to buy blackout materials during the war: it was where you went to get things you weren't meant to get. **Rationing** began in 1940. The idea was that everyone got a share of basic necessities, but no more than that. In actual fact, you could normally buy extra on the illegal 'black market' if you had the money. Farmers and shopkeepers would sell extra supplies of rationed food 'under the counter'. **Spivs** arranged to sell black market petrol or cigarettes in pubs.

The police tried their best to crack down on the black market. Before March 1942, when private motoring was completely banned, they sometimes put red dye in the petrol which was meant for doctors or farmers - and others who needed it for their work. If the police found coloured petrol in your car when it wasn't meant to be there, you were in deep trouble.

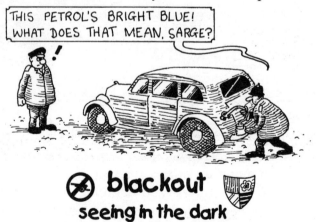

⊘ blackout
seeing in the dark

It was difficult for bombers to find the way to their targets at night. Usually they had to follow rivers which reflected moonlight and the paler light of the sky, or railway lines which also showed up well.

Blackout regulations in most European countries meant that they couldn't steer by looking out for car headlights, traffic lights, street lights, house lights - or any man-made lights at all.

In Britain, all windows had to be covered in dark material. Not a chink of light was allowed to show. If it did, the **air raid warden** would be on to you. Torches, which were needed because there were no street lights, had to be covered in tissue paper. Buses and trains were darkened so that you had to grope your way to your seat. Perhaps worst of all, car headlights were covered except for a very thin slit which allowed just a sliver of light to light the road. Road accidents doubled. 4,000 people died from them during the war, which was a lot considering how few cars there were by modern standards.

Blitz
when Britain was bombed
1940-41

'Blitz' is the name given to the German bombing campaign of Britain during the early stages of World

War II. The word comes from the German *blitzkrieg* meaning 'lightning war'. During the course of the Blitz, the Germans dropped 27,500 tons of high explosives on Britain, killing around 61,000 people and injuring another 100,000. The worst of it was over by May 1941. After that, the Germans concentrated on Russia. At its peak, between August 1940 and May 1941, German air raids were almost non-stop. In London people almost forgot what it was like to go to sleep without being woken by air raid sirens. London took the brunt of the bombing but all Britain's major industrial cities were badly hit.

Blitzkrieg
plunder and lightning

Blitzkrieg, meaning 'lightning war', was the name used by the Germans to describe their tactics at the start of the war. They were the first to realise that aircraft used with tanks and other motorised transport could make war happen much faster than in the past. Lightning attacks could destroy an enemy before the enemy had time to organise a fight back. This was what happened to Poland in 1939 and to France in 1940. But *Blitzkrieg* failed against the Russians in **Operation Barbarossa**. Russia was just too big for a lightning war. Later, all armies used similar tactics when it was possible.

22

Braun, Eva ♀
Adolf's little friend

1910-45

Eva Braun was the daughter of a German schoolteacher. In 1930 she was working in a photographer's shop in southern Germany when who should walk in but - **Adolf Hitler**! She became his mistress and in 1936 he installed her in his hilltop hideaway, the *Berghof*, a chalet/villa in Berchtesgarden in southern Germany, otherwise called the 'Eagle's Nest'.

70

In 1945 when Germany was on the edge of total defeat, Eva joined Hitler in his concrete

'*Führerbunker*' beneath central Berlin. Although he'd told her not to come, she wanted to be with him in his final hours. They were married on 29 April 1945. Next day she poisoned herself and Hitler either poisoned himself or shot himself beside her body.

Britain, Battle of
when the *Luftwaffe* lost it
1940

The Battle of Britain was the first battle ever to be fought entirely in the air. It was fought in beautiful blue skies over southern Britain in the summer of
70 1940. After the British retreat from Dunkirk, **Hitler** had planned that the all-conquering German army would invade Britain along the south coast. Britain would crumble within a couple of weeks, or so he thought. There was just one tiny problem - before the invasion (called 'Operation Sealion') could start, the German Airforce or *Luftwaffe* had to defeat the
100 **Royal Air Force**. If not, British planes would be able to bomb the German invasion barges. At first, the Germans attacked air fields, factories and ports.

47 Air Chief Marshal **Hugh Dowding**, head of British Fighter Command, was ready. By 1939, new Spitfire and Hurricane fighters were being built in large

numbers. A shield of radar stations had been set up around the coasts of Britain, ready to feed back information on the numbers and lines of attack of German planes, so that the new British fighters could be 'scrambled' to cut them off. Radar, then a new technology, was to be the eyes and ears of the British defence.

TAKE THE ONE ON THE LEFT, SMITHERS!

ROGER, WING COMMANDER!

The Battle of Britain began in earnest on 13 August, *Adlertag* ('Eagle Day'), as **Hermann Goering**, commander of the *Luftwaffe*, called it. At the start of the Battle of Britain, the odds were very much against the British. They had just 900 fighters, of which only 600 could be expected to be in the air at any one time. Against this the Germans had 1,260 long range bombers and 1,320 dive bombers in total, with a force of 1,080 fighter planes to protect them. Although, to be fair, quite a number of the German planes were based too far away to be of much use. More importantly, Dowding understood something vital: all that was necessary was for Britain *not to lose* the battle - so long as the **RAF** still existed, Hitler could not afford to start Operation Sealion and launch his invasion fleet across the Channel.

As it turned out, the main problem for the British wasn't a lack of planes but a lack of trained pilots. The young heroes who flew the Spitfires and

Hurricanes spent most of the battle in a daze of exhaustion, because there was so little time for them to recover between sorties.

Of course, during late August and early September, no one knew that the Germans would lose. It looked for a while as if they might win. Then on 7 September, Goering made a very foolish mistake. He switched the focus of his attack to massive bombing raids on London - the start of the **Blitz**. This was bad for the people of London but good for the RAF, because it gave them a breather. A breather was all they needed. On 15 September, 'Battle of Britain Day', Fighter Command claimed to have shot down 185 enemy planes. Even the mighty *Luftwaffe* couldn't cope with losses like that, not on a daily basis. Two days later, **Hitler** decided to postpone Operation Sealion indefinitely. The Blitz continued but the threat of invasion had gone and the Battle of Britain was over.

Bulge, Battle of *see* **Ardennes, Battle of**

Burma-Thailand Railway
eastern engineering project

By 1942, the Japanese had won control of a large chunk of southern Asia, but they didn't have enough ships to supply their armies in all those parts and anyway ships were always in danger of attack by Allied warships. They decided to build a railway line through the jungles of eastern Thailand into Burma. This would create a safe overland supply route to the Indian Ocean.

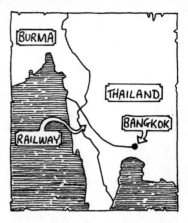

The railway was begun in July 1942 and completed in October 1943. It wound for 420 kilometres (260 miles) through thick jungle and mountains. It was an engineering feat - and it was also a crime. The Japanese used 61,000 British, Australian and Dutch prisoners of war together with 270,000 Asians as slave labourers to build their railway. They treated them like animals. Starvation diet, appalling living conditions and sheer, brutal, forced labour took their toll. 12,000 Allied POWs and 90,000 Asian labourers died before the project was finished. As it turned out, the railway was less useful than the Japanese had expected. Allied bombing destroyed sections of it in 1944, including the famous bridge over the River Kwai. It was abandoned in 1945.

Chamberlain, Neville
P.M. who promised peace
1869-1940

Neville Chamberlain was a rather quiet man who became Prime Minister in 1937. By then, **Hitler**, who was a very noisy man, was demanding *lebensraum* ('living space') for the German people - and threatening war if he didn't get it.

Chamberlain tried to negotiate a peaceful agreement with Hitler. He seems not to have understood the sort of monster he was dealing with. In the German city of Munich, on 30 September 1938, the two men signed an agreement which allowed Hitler to take over the Sudetenland, a large chunk of Czechoslovakia. Returning home, Chamberlain waved

82 his copy of the '**Munich Agreement**' and told vast, relieved crowds in London that he had brought them 'peace in our time'.

As it turned out, Chamberlain had appeased Hitler but he hadn't stopped him. The monster was greedy for more. In March, Hitler invaded the rest of

42 **Czechoslovakia** and in September 1939 he attacked

92 **Poland**. Britain was forced to go to war anyway.

Chamberlain resigned from office after the British army was forced to retreat from Norway in May 1940. His policy of 'appeasement' was in ruins. It had

35 always been condemned by his successor, **Winston Churchill**. To be fair to Chamberlain, appeasement had bought Britain a short breathing space in which to re-arm and prepare for war.

Churchill, Winston
baby-faced British bulldog

1874-1965

In his blue siren suit, (dungarees, which he had designed specially) and with his balding head, Winston Churchill looked like a great big baby in rompers, a baby with a large cigar. He was outrageous. At the height of the **Blitz** he was everywhere, in the bombed out streets, in the war office, on the radio, urging the British people to stand firm. The siren suit, the large cigar, the V for victory sign were all part of an image. With a leader like me, Churchill was saying, the British must be the complete opposite of Nazi Germany - where men in shiny boots rule ruthlessly.

Churchill became Prime Minister in 1940, when **Chamberlain** resigned following the British retreat from Norway. He immediately put Britain on a full war footing and set an example by working incredibly hard. It took a gang of secretaries to keep up with him. On a typical working day he would spend most of the morning in bed, dictating letters and orders or reading reports, then he would get up for meetings, then followed a champagne lunch and a two hour nap. After the nap there would be further meetings or office work and then a long dinner - and after dinner he went back to work or plunged into discussions with his staff until the early hours of the morning. All this was fuelled by whisky and cigars. He was exhausting.

When asked what Churchill did during the war, one of his generals said that 'he talked about it'. Which was true. Churchill wrote brilliant speeches. But he also poked his nose into all kinds of details. In 1943, a memo to his Minister of Agriculture said:

> *... you have discontinued the small sugar ration which was allowed to bees, and which is most important to their work throughout the whole year.*

One of Churchill's main aims was to persuade America to enter the war. He knew that Britain was too small to win on her own. He once greeted 99 **Roosevelt** while standing naked in his bath, saying:

> *The Prime Minister of Britain has nothing to hide from the President of the United States.*

When the war was over, the British people voted Churchill out of office. He was a war leader. Now they wanted a peace leader. Churchill was hurt but 70 he accepted the vote. Unlike **Hitler**, he believed in democracy.

civil defence
they fought for life

Before the war started, the British government calculated that each ton of high explosive dropped by German bombers would kill an average of fifty people. That meant around two million dead. Up to 5,500,000 square metres of coffin timber would be needed, or cardboard if timber was too expensive. As part of this planning, an air raid warden service was set up in 1937. More than half a million people joined it following the **Munich Crisis** of 1938.

82

Civil Defence meant just that: civilians who worked to defend civilians, all the brave people who kept British cities going during the terror of the **Blitz**. It included air raid wardens, rescue and stretcher parties, messenger boys and staff to man the control centres. Then there were the medical services, including ambulance drivers, and staff to man the first aid posts. Finally there were the fire services.

27

At the height of the Blitz all these people worked themselves into a state of exhaustion. Rescue parties dug into the rubble to bring out the bodies of the

dead or to save the wounded. Ambulance men or stretcher parties took the wounded away through the rubble-strewn streets to the first aid posts or hospitals where they would be patched up. Firemen worked frantically to put out the flames. In total about 1.5 million people were involved in civil defence - which doesn't include the many thousand 120 members of the **WVS** who did vital work and the thousands who manned observation posts day and night, watching for enemy bombers which might come in below radar height.

⊘ clothes
things people wore in wartime

Shabby man in single-breasted suit with no turn-ups seeks shabby woman with gravy on her legs.

If World War II lonely-hearts adverts had been honest, that was the sort of thing they would have 95 had to say. Clothes **rationing** came in in June 1941. After that it was very difficult to buy new clothes. Shabbiness became a way of life during the war. Because fashionable nylon stockings were in short supply, many women pretended that they were wearing them by painting gravy browning or tea on their legs instead. The law said that men's suits had to be single-breasted with no turn-ups on the trousers so as to save material. The number of pockets was also limited.

People had to 'make do and mend'. Socks were darned again and again. Jumpers were unravelled and new ones knitted from the wool. Women made dresses from curtain material, and underwear from parachute silk - if they were lucky enough to get hold of any.

Despite the rationing you could still buy some good quality 'utility' clothes. These were made to good basic standards from good simple materials. Often they were designed by top designers as part of the war effort. And they were quite cheap.

⊗ collaborators
people who helped the enemy

During the war, 'collaboration' meant 'helping the enemy' or 'working for him'. All the German-occupied countries had their collaborators. In fact, to start with, when it looked as if Germany was going to win, most people collaborated a little because they thought there was no choice. But real, serious collaborators went out of their way to help the Germans, either for money or power or because they too were fascists and agreed with what Germany was doing. The police forces of Holland and **Vichy France**, for instance, helped to round up Jews to be

40 put on trains to German **concentration camps**. Only Poland had no collaborators worth speaking of.

After the war was over, many collaborators were punished. 35,000 were tried and found guilty in Belgium. In France, women who had had affairs with German soldiers had their heads shaved and were booed in the streets.

concentration camps
pure evil

The Nazis opened their first concentration camps, including Dachau, back in 1933 as soon as they came to power. Next year, the *Totenkopfverbüde* (Deaths-Head Battalions) had been set up by the SS to run them.

On the whole, concentration camps were different to the extermination camps used to murder Jews in the Final Solution, which were mainly in Poland. Concentration camp prisoners included criminals, gypsies, communists and other opponents of the regime, as well as Jews.

The number of prisoners grew and grew, especially after the invasions of Poland and Russia. Inmates weren't exterminated as such, but they suffered horribly and many were killed anyway. 22,000 Russian officers were executed in Sachsenhausen, in 1942. At several camps, especially the extermination camps, including Auschwitz and Dachau, the Nazis performed medical experiments on living prisoners.

However, most of the prisoners died of overwork or starvation. This was because they were used as slave labour for German industry and were paid in food. If they didn't work they didn't eat and often they were too weak to work - due to overwork. The prisoners were often kept in small camps close to the factories. German businesses, including major names which are still around today, paid the government for the slave labour. The system reached a peak in 1944.

The first concentration camp to be liberated by the Allies was Buchenwald, on 11 April 1945. Photographs of the starving inmates, more like skeletons than people, were the first glimpse given to the outside world of the true horror of the Nazi system. Probably around 600,000 died in the concentration camps.

CONVOYS *see* **Atlantic, Battle of**

Czechoslovakia, invasion of
Hitler's first victim
1939

Before the war, Czechoslovakia was a lamb and Germany was a great, big, slavering wolf. Czechoslovakia was a smallish country of fourteen million people; the population of Germany was 79.5 million, and three million of the Czechs were Germans anyway. These Czech Germans lived in an area nextdoor to Germany called the **Sudetenland**. Under the **Munich Agreement** of September 1938, signed by **Neville Chamberlain** and **Hitler**, the Germans were allowed to take control of the Sudetenland. At the same time, Poland took a slice of northern Czechoslovakia and Hungary took a slice of the east. There wasn't that much left. The Germans gobbled up the rest in an armed invasion launched on 15 March 1939.

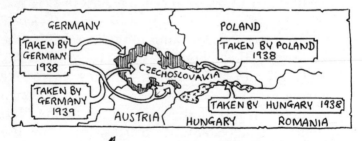

Dambusters
when bombs bounced

The Ruhr Valley was the smoky, industrial heartland of wartime Germany. From the factories of the Ruhr poured countless tanks, guns and planes to feed the German war machine. The Dambusters' raid was a clever scheme by the **RAF** to hit the Ruhr Valley by damaging the water supply.

'Dambusters' was the name given to RAF 617 Squadron which would carry out the attack. Engineer and designer Barnes Wallis had developed a special 'bouncing bomb' to destroy the Ruhr dams. If dropped on water at the correct height and speed, it would bounce like a skimming stone, hit its dam, roll down the dam wall and explode near the bottom. The correct height for dropping was just eighteen metres (60 feet). The Dambusters had to be superb pilots. Nineteen bombers set out on the night of 16-17 of May 1943. Eleven came back. The scheme worked. They struck two massive dams causing widespread flooding.

☞ D-Day
the beginning of the end
6 June 1944

In the early hours of 6 June 1944, 23,400 US and British paratroopers were dropped from the sky into the darkened countryside of Normandy, in German-occupied France. Their job was to seize strategic bridges and other points in advance of the Allied invasion force, which was to be the largest sea-borne invasion force the world has ever seen.

D-Day had begun.

Planning for the invasion of German-occupied Europe had begun back in January 1943. The codename for the whole operation was 'Overlord' and the overall commander was the American General **Eisenhower**, 'Ike' as he was known. There'd been a huge, two-year build-up of Allied troops and armour in Britain, which became like a giant aircraft carrier moored to the European coast.

As D-Day itself approached, German defences and communications were pounded by Allied bombers and sabotaged by members of the French **resistance**. They hit targets all along the coast so that the Germans were kept guessing as to where the invasion forces would land. The actual invasion area was to be the coast of Normandy, in France.

The day was planned for 5 June but had to be put off for twenty-four hours due to bad weather. Once it began, the sky above southern Britain was darkened by endless streams of Allied warplanes heading south. The roads were clogged with thousands of vehicles carrying men to the invasion fleet.

Meanwhile the sea off Normandy was already full of Allied ships. There was a massive naval bombardment. Finally, although still early in the morning, the invasion force landed on five beaches to the west of the town of Caen. 75,215 British and Canadian troops and 57,500 Americans were landed on the first day. The German defences included underwater obstacles, concrete gun positions and
10 minefields, and the **Allies**, particularly the Americans, took heavy casualties. But they pushed inland and more soldiers poured onto the beaches behind them. Two floating, concrete 'Mulberry' harbours were towed across the Channel and sunk in position to speed up the process of unloading tanks, men and other equipment. D-Day was over - the Battle of Normandy had begun.

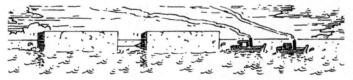

De Gaulle, Charles
first of the Free Frenchmen
1890-1970

Charles de Gaulle was very tall and he had a very long nose. He tended to look down it. He certainly wasn't going to look up it at the Germans. When France fell in 1940, French leader Marshal Pétain asked the Germans for an armistice*. De Gaulle was just a junior government minister at the time, but unlike other ministers he refused to bow down.
100 Instead, he was smuggled out of France in an **RAF**

plane. Once in London, he broadcast messages of defiance by radio. He was recognised by the British as the 'leader of all free Frenchmen'. From that time on, he and his supporters were known as the 'Free French'.

De Gaulle was a prickly, difficult man. France was all he really cared about and it was very difficult for him to accept help from the British. But he had no choice, and his most important backer was always **Winston Churchill**. The American President, **Franklin Roosevelt**, would have dropped de Gaulle like a shot if he could, because he loathed him. The reason he didn't was down to Churchill.

De Gaulle's great moment came on 26 August 1944 when he entered Paris at the head of the first forces of liberation. A vast crowd of Parisians roared their greeting. He was President of France until January 1946 and again from 1958-69.

VIVE LA FRANCE!

digging for victory *see* **rationing**

doodle-bugs *see* **flying bombs**

Dowding, Air Chief Marshal Sir Hugh 'Stuffy'

he commanded fighters

1882-1970

Hugh Dowding's officers called him 'Stuffy' because he was serious and old fashioned. But when it came to air warfare, he was anything but old fashioned - and deadly serious. He was in charge of British air defences from 1936 right through to 1940, as Commander-in-Chief of Fighter Command. Due to Dowding more than anyone else, in 1939 when the war started, Fighter Command had squadrons of the very latest Spitfire and Hurricane fighters and a chain of brand new radar stations around the coast to warn of enemy attack. Radar was a very new technology.

49 In the dark days following the retreat from **Dunkirk**, Dowding understood that, whatever happened, Fighter Command must not be defeated. If they

could just stay in the skies then the Germans would be unable to launch their invasion army, which was waiting just across the English Channel. That was what the **Battle of Britain** was all about. The British were outgunned so Dowding looked after his hard-stretched men and planes very carefully. Others complained that he was overcautious, but his strategy worked.

30

Dowding was sacked from his job in November 1940. A poor reward for what he'd done. Nowadays his name is remembered with gratitude.

THERE, THERE DEAR, YOU DID YOUR BIT.

🔸 Dresden, bombing of
beautiful city blasted by bombs
1944

The German city of Dresden was once known as the 'Florence of the North' and was reckoned to be one of the most beautiful cities in the world. On the night of 13-14 February 1944, two waves of nearly eight hundred British bombers roared out of the dark sky above it. They dropped 1,478 tons of high explosive and 1,182 tons of fire bombs. The fire bombs started a 'fire storm' at the heart of the city. Hot air rising from the burning buildings drew in gales of cooler air beneath which fanned the flames still further. Next day, a raid by 311 US B17 bombers added to the carnage. Dresden was never a major industrial city so the aim of the raids was pure terror, to 'break the will' of the German people, as **Bomber Harris** put it, and to back up Russian efforts fighting the Germans in the east.

Further raids against Dresden went on until April 17. By that time the city was flattened. Estimates of how many died run from 35,000 to 135,000. It's likely that more died than in all the German raids on Britain put together.

✕ Dunkirk 🚢
a narrow escape
1940

In May 1940, the British and French armies were falling back through Belgium before the victorious German armies. Soon they were penned into a small area of land around the port of Dunkirk in northern France. They were like sheep in a sheepfold waiting for slaughter.

Between 26 May and 3 June, 338,000 men were rescued from Dunkirk beach. Ships and boats of all shapes and sizes took them off. Fortunately the water

was calm, so even quite small leisure boats were able
to help. But whenever the weather and the **RAF**
allowed it, the dive bombers of the *Luftwaffe* struck
mercilessly. Dark plumes of smoke rose above
stricken ships - smoke which at least gave cover to
other ships. Meanwhile the pilots of the RAF, flying
from bases in England, fought back bravely. They
were heavily outnumbered and lost 177 planes, but
their support was vital - as was a delay in pressing
home the attack by the commander of the German
forces, General von Rundstedt.

Dunkirk was a defeat and caused bitterness between
the British and the French because the French had
wanted to stay and fight and because the British took
off many of their own men first. But it was a *glorious*
defeat according to **Churchill**. Basically, **Hitler** had
had the chance to capture the entire British army and
he'd muffed it. If he'd captured all the men who
escaped, he might have been able to invade Britain
shortly after, and if he'd done that - he might have
won the war.

Eisenhower, Dwight David
🎖 'Ike'
American general who took command
1890-1969

General Eisenhower, or 'Ike' as he was fondly known by the public, was appointed Supreme Commander of all Allied forces in western Europe in 1944. His job was to lead the combined British, American, Canadian, Free French, Polish and all the others as they massed for the great **D-Day** invasion of German-occupied Europe. It was Ike who decided on the final date for the invasion and who was top commander when the massive Allied forces pushed forward through France and into Germany itself.

Ike was clever and a brilliant soldier but he was also cheerful and popular. He insisted that all the different nationalities in his huge army got on reasonably well with each other. His officers could call each other 'sons of bitches' if they wanted to, 'but he was damned if he would have them calling each other 'British or American sons of bitches''.

✗ El Alamein
danger in the desert
1942

El Alamein is a dreary desert railway halt in northern Egypt. It's also the scene of two key battles in the fight for North Africa during World War II.

51

In the summer of 1942, General **Rommel's** *panzer* army was advancing east across North Africa. The British retreated before it. It seemed only a matter of time before the Germans captured the Suez Canal which was the main route to their Japanese allies in the Far East. El Alamein was where the British with their Australian and New Zealand friends stopped Rommel in his tracks (1-4 July 1942).

In the second Battle of El Alamein (23 October - 4 November 1942), the British and their allies counter-
attacked under General **Montgomery**. Rommel was short of fuel for his tanks and he had to fight defensively, which wasn't his style. And he was also outnumbered. After a fierce twelve day fight, the Allies broke through. They drove the Germans all the way back to Tunisia, taking 30,000 prisoners in the process.

Enigma machine
devious coding device

During the 1930s, the German armed forces developed a special machine for sending messages in code. They believed that messages sent in code by their 'Enigma' machine were uncrackable. Each encoded letter might stand for any one of over a hundred million possible alternatives. It would take a lifetime to decode one letter.

But there were chinks in the Enigma mystery. Among others: a coded letter could never stand for itself, i.e. if the receiver read the letter 'A' in code, he or she knew that it *didn't* stand for 'A'. By 1938, a team of brilliant, young Polish mathematicians had cracked the code and built their own primitive Enigma-cracking machine, codenamed *Bomba* after a type of ice cream. The Poles passed their information on to France and Britain the following year when Poland was about to fall to the Germans.

After the fall of France as well as Poland, the torch of decipherment passed firmly into British hands. Operation **ULTRA**, the codename for information got from enigma messages, gathered a team of world-class mathematicians and government experts at a secret location at Bletchley Park in the Midlands. Among other things, ULTRA developed the first modern computer, called 'Colossus', under the direction of the brilliant mathematician Alan Turing. Colossus churned through all the millions of possibilities that an Enigma message might represent, taking hours to do what would have taken human beings weeks or months.

Operation ULTRA was worth armies. It did as much as anything to win the war for the **Allies**. The Germans never knew that their most vital messages were being read, even messages from **Adolf Hitler** about where to send his forces. The men and women who worked for ULTRA were so clever and so honest that their work remained a secret for twenty-nine years after the war was over.

ENSA

(Entertainments National Service Association)
travelling troupe of troop cheerers

ENSA ('E-very N-ight S-omething A-wful' as people joked) was set up to provide entertainment for the British armed forces. The idea was to cheer service people up by putting on special travelling shows for them. Some ENSA performers escaped with the troops from **Dunkirk**. Later, ENSA put on shows in factory canteens as well.

🚫 evacuation
when the children left home

Poor little children ill treated by horrid host families in villages far from home. Happy little children making new friends in the countryside and playing with the lambs and piglets: for some children, evacuation - the mass movement of children to safe areas away from bombs and bullets - was dreadful, for others it was wonderful.

Before the war started, the government knew that children in the big cities would be in danger from German bombs. Once war was declared (September 1939), a mass 'evacuation' began immediately. 827,000 school-age children, 103,000 teachers, 524,000 toddlers with their mothers and 12,000 pregnant women were moved to the countryside. Nothing like it had ever happened in Britain before. The stations were crowded with children, each carrying a **gas mask** and either a bag or a brown paper parcel with spare clothes in it. When they reached their destinations, the children were taken to the local school or church hall and there shared out among the locals.

Middle class hosts were often shocked by the poverty of evacuees who came from slum areas. Some children had never slept in a bed before or brushed their teeth or even used a knife and fork. It was an eye-opener all round.

WHY SHOULD I BRUSH MY TEETH? THEY'RE NOT HAIRY!

The big evacuation happened in the summer of 1939. But when winter came round, still no bombs had dropped (this being the **Phoney War** period). Many parents took their children back home to the cities. This meant that when the **Blitz** finally started the following September, lots of children were in the danger zones - and their schools were in the countryside because many of the schools had been evacuated along with the children.

WELCOME HOME!

91

27

In 1945, when the Blitz was just a memory, the flying bombs started. There was a second mass evacuation from the main cities, although not nearly as big as the first one.

fascists *see* **Nazi Party** *and* **Mussolini, Benito**

☜☞ Final Solution
what Hitler did to the Jews

The Nazis believed that north Europeans, Germans in particular, were a master race, destined to rule the world. German Jews were spots of pollution on the pure German soil. They must be got rid of, along with gypsies, homosexuals, disabled people and opponents of the regime.

70 **Hitler** tried several 'solutions' to the *Judenfrage*, the Jewish question as he called it. Firstly, from 1933 when he came to power, Jews (meaning anyone with at least a Jewish grandparent) were forced to leave small German towns and villages and to gather in the cities. Then, from 1933 to 1939 when the war started and it became impossible, Jews were 'encouraged' to emigrate. Half of all German Jews had left by 1938.

When the Germans conquered most of Europe they also conquered several million more European Jews. Starting in 1941, they began mass killings of Jews in newly-conquered lands in the east. Whole Jewish communities, some numbering tens of thousands, were murdered. The killing squads sent back reports of numbers killed on a daily or weekly basis.

The mass killings were horrific but still there were lots of Jews left over. In the autumn of 1941, Adolf Eichmann was put in charge of the 'Race and Resettlement Office'. It was his job to work out details of a 'Final Solution' to the 'Jewish Question' - there wouldn't be any more solutions after this one because there wouldn't be any Jews left to solve.

That autumn the Germans experimented with gassing Russian prisoners of war and a few Jews. The Final Solution was to be the mass murder by gas of all Jews remaining in German hands. They were to be collected from their home countries, if possible by the local police, held in local camps and then sent by train, either monthly or weekly, to **concentration camps** in remote parts of eastern Europe far away from any major cities. And so it was.

It's been estimated that eleven million people were murdered by the Nazis and around six million of them were Jewish (as defined by the Nazis) - about a third of the total world population of Jews in 1939. This dreadful crime is now known as the 'Holocaust'.

🚀 flying bombs
they bugged the British

In 1944, as the Allied armies fought their way ever deeper into German-occupied Europe, **Hitler** boasted of a special, secret weapon which would change the course of the war. This secret weapon was the flying bomb. The first of them to fall on England (on 13 June 1944 a week after **D-Day**) was a V-1 bomb, called a 'Doodle-bug' or 'buzz' bomb by the British. Doodle-bugs flew at around 600 kph. It was when the engine cut out that you had to worry, because that was when the bomb plunged to earth. Doodle-bugs killed around 6,000 people before the war was over. They were hard to shoot down but not impossible. Sometimes pilots would fly alongside and tip a wing under them. The destabilised bomb then spiralled out of control.

The V-2 was a more advanced weapon. With its rocket engine, it flew at a maximum speed of 5,793 kph (3,600 mph) and was impossible to shoot down. The first V-2 was launched at Britain on 8 September 1944. V-2s killed around 3,000 people.

Around 10,000 flying bombs were launched in total.

food *see* **rationing**

Free French *see* **De Gaulle, Charles**

🚫 gas masks 🛡
a breath of stale air

Before World War II started, people were very frightened that the Germans would drop poison gas bombs. Poison gas had caused terrible injuries during World War I. Towards the end of that war, a quarter of all artillery shells fired had been poison gas shells. If not killed, victims were often blinded or had damaged lungs.

In 1939, the government issued gas masks to all British citizens. Everyone had to practise putting them on. They were very uncomfortable and there tended to be a build up of spit and sweat in the bottom if you wore your mask for any length of time. Babies were given special masks which covered their entire cot and there were even gas masks for some favourite horses and household pets. They became a bit of a fashion item - for the better off, at any rate. You could tell the posh kids because they carried their masks in leather cases rather than the standard canvas ones.

LOOK AT SMARTY PANTS WITH HIS *LEATHER* CASE!

Fortunately gas masks were never needed. Both sides produced plenty of poison gas, just in case, but neither side wanted to be the first to use it.

♀ G.I. brides ⊘
they loved Americans

43   In the build-up towards **D-Day**, over a million US troops were stationed in Britain. Their uniforms looked better than the uniforms of the British soldiers and they were paid three times as much. This meant that they tended to be popular with the local girls. They could afford to give their girlfriends presents of cigarettes, scented soap and nylon stockings, which they bought from their own Post Exchange stores in their camps. American soldiers were called 'GIs' from the words 'government issue' which were stamped on their clothing. (Less politely,

it was said to come from 'Galvanized Iron' - from their garbage cans.) When the war was over and the GIs returned home, they took 60,000 'GI brides' back home with them.

Goebbels, Joseph
he limped behind his leader

1897-1945

Joseph Goebbels limped. He had a club foot and may have been teased at school, which perhaps explains his bitter attitude towards the world and towards Jews in particular. He joined the **Nazi Party** in the 1920s and became their **propaganda** chief, building up **Hitler's** image as an honest German who cared for his country. Without Goebbels, Hitler might never have come to power. It was Goebbels who started the fashion for saying 'Heil Hitler' all the time and giving the Nazi salute. It was also Goebbels who first referred to Hitler as his '*Führer*'. Goebbels became one of the most important men in Nazi Germany.

84
93
70

In April 1945 when enemy forces were fighting their way into the very heart of Berlin, Goebbels joined Hitler in the *Führerbunker* beneath the city. There he witnessed Hitler's marriage to Eva Braun. Hitler and Eva committed suicide the next day. The day after that, Goebbels had his own children poisoned by a Nazi colonel. Goebbels and Mrs Goebbels then committed suicide.

Goering, Hermann
lumpish Luftwaffe leader

1893-1946

Hermann Goering (or 'Göring'), a World War I fighter ace, joined the **Nazi Party** in 1922, three years after **Hitler**. Next year he was wounded in the 'Beer Hall Putsch', a Nazi attempt to seize power in southern Germany. He became addicted to morphine which he took to stop the pain. In the early stages of the war he was the most powerful man in the country after Hitler and it was said of him that he was more of a Nazi than Hitler himself. He ordered the opening of the first **concentration camps** and started the dreaded secret police, the Gestapo. It was Goering who had signed the decree ordering a '**Final Solution**' to the Jewish question.

Among his other jobs, Goering was head of the *Luftwaffe*. Defeat in the **Battle of Britain** and the failure of the **Blitz** along with other failures meant that he gradually lost power as the war went on. He became a rather silly, overweight figure travelling between luxury homes with a nurse and his personal doctor in his luxury private train, called *Asia*. A lover of luxury, on occasion he would greet people dressed in a purple dressing gown, stinking of perfume and with rouge on his cheeks. He looted precious paintings from all over Europe.

DO COME INTO MY TRAIN.

When the war ended, other top Nazis had fled or were dead. Goering was left as the most important
Nazi in the **Nuremberg trials**. He poisoned himself with cyanide a few hours before he was due to be executed.

Harris, Sir Arthur
'Bomber Harris'
he believed in bombing
1892-1984

Arthur Harris was Commander-in-Chief of British Bomber Command from 1942-45. He believed that 'area bombing' of German cities could break the will of the German people and thus help win the war for
the **Allies**. An odd idea since the Germans had tried
the same thing on Britain during the **Blitz** and it had had the opposite effect. He also believed that fire

bombs could be more destructive than ordinary explosives and set out to prove the point with 'saturation bombing' of the medieval city of Lübeck, on 28 March 1942. Lübeck was mainly built of wood, 'more like a firelighter than a human habitation'. It was duly destroyed.

Shortly after Lübeck, on 30 May 1942, Harris ordered the first 'thousand bomber' raid, on the city of Cologne. Many more 'thousand bomber' raids followed. In another raid on Cologne on 28 July 1943, a fire storm raised temperatures in the city centre to over 1000°C. Whole trees were sucked from the ground by the updraft. Charred adult bodies shrank to the size of children and children to the size of dolls. 40,000 died - more than in all the bombing of Britain by Germany during the war.

Harris was also involved in the destruction of Dresden on 13 February 1945. People still argue about him. His method certainly weakened Germany by drawing fighter planes away from the war fronts to defend the cities, but it was very expensive in human life - the lives of his own pilots as well as German civilians.

Haw Haw, Lord *see* Joyce, William

Heydrich, Reinhard
'the hangman'
sinister secret police supremo
1904-42

Reinhard Heydrich was tall, blond and handsome, a member of the 'Master Race' if ever there was one. He was a cruel and ruthless Nazi who rose to become head of the Gestapo and all the other secret police organisations of the Nazi state. It was Heydrich who 57 pushed for ruthless completion of the **'Final Solution'** to the 'Jewish Question' at a conference held at Wannsee, near Berlin, in January 1942. It was to be called 'Operation Reinhard' in his honour. He was blown up in his car by two Free Czech agents in Czechoslovakia on 27 May 1942. The agents had 102 been trained by the **Special Operations Executive** in

Britain and were parachuted in to do the job. The agents, plus 1,300 innocent Czechs, were killed by the Nazis in retaliation for his death.

Himmler, Heinrich
a very nasty Nazi
1900-45

In 1929, Heinrich Himmler was made head of the SS (*Shutzstaffeln*, meaning 'protection squads'). At that 70 time the SS were **Hitler's** troop of personal thugs - bodyguards to put it more politely. Himmler

developed the SS into a powerful force. He was its
head from 1929 right through to his death at the end
of the war in 1945. It was Himmler who set up the
40 first **concentration camp**, for opponents of the
regime, at Dachau in March 1933. Later he became
Minister of the Interior and 'Reichs Commissioner
for the Strengthening of German Nationhood'. As
57 such, he was political head of the '**Final Solution**'.

In 1945, realising that Germany had lost the war,
Himmler tried to negotiate
10 a peace deal with the **Allies**
behind Hitler's back, but
the Allies were having none of it.
He fled Berlin in disguise after
Germany surrendered but was
captured by British troops. He
poisoned himself by
biting into a cyanide capsule
which he'd hidden in his
mouth.

ZE COAST EEZ CLEAR.
I SHALL FLEE!

Hirohito, Emperor and god
mildish Japanese monarch

1901-89

Hirohito was the 124th Emperor of Japan by direct
descent. He came to the throne in 1926 when his
reign was given the official name 'Showa' -
'Enlightened Peace'. The first half of the reign was
the opposite of peaceful. At that time the Japanese
government was dominated by the army, and the
army wanted to carve out a Japanese empire in the

Far East. Probably Hirohito would have liked to avoid war, but he had little real power - even though, officially, he was a god.

When the war was over, Hirohito offered to take personal responsibility for the horrendous crimes committed by Japanese forces. The American General **MacArthur** refused to accept this. He knew that Hirohito was not as bad as the worst of the Japanese generals and that Hirohito had only ever wanted to be a constitutional monarch along the lines of British Kings and Queens. Hirohito gave up being a god in 1946 - he'd never believed in it anyway. He ruled for another forty-three (peaceful) years - so he got his Showa in the end.

Hiroshima
A-bomb and not just a bomb
August 1945

By August 1945, Germany had surrendered and Japan had as good as lost the war in the east. There was just one problem - the Japanese army refused to surrender. They were determined to fight to the bitter end, which would have caused horrendous casualties both for the Japanese and for the Americans who were fighting them. The American answer to this problem was equally horrendous - the atom bomb.

The first nuclear bomb to be dropped in anger was released from an American B29 bomber at 08.15 on 6 August 1945. It was 3 metres long and weighed 3,600 kg (8,000 lbs). 'Little Boy' fell towards the city of Hiroshima by parachute and exploded at a height of 580 metres (1,885 ft) for maximum damage. At least 70,000 people died immediately or very soon after from their wounds. The final death toll including deaths from radiation may be as high as 140,000. A second bomb, called 'Fat Boy', was dropped three days later on the city of Nagasaki and up to another 80,000 were killed.

The atom bombs had the desired effect. They shocked the Japanese army into agreeing to surrender. The war in the east came to an end on 14 August when the Japanese high command at last agreed to surrender unconditionally.

Hitler, Adolf
bad artist; good murderer
1889-1945

Adolf Hitler, born Adolf Schicklgruber, was the son of an Austrian customs official. When young he wanted to be an artist and led a lonely life in Vienna trying to earn his living by painting postcards among other things. When World War I started he was happy to give up this life and to join the German army. Now he wasn't lonely any more.

Hitler was a brave soldier and won a medal. When World War I ended, he was once again at a loose end and missed his army pals. Next year he joined what was soon to become the **Nazi Party**, so now he wasn't alone again.

More importantly, he was a political genius. Two years later (1921) he was the Nazi leader. His political ideas are spelled out in his book, *Mein Kampf* (*My Struggle*) written in prison following a failed push for power in Bavaria (the Beer Hall Putsch) in southern Germany. His ideas are ignorant and unpleasant. He was an out and out racist who believed in the superiority of the German '*volk*' (people) and had a special hatred for Jews.

In 1933, the Nazi Party took power. Hitler was now absolute leader (*Führer*) of Germany. Within months, all opposition was crushed and the Nazi programme of dominating Europe and getting rid of the Jews was about to begin. Several people tried to kill him during the war. **Colonel von Stauffenberg** came closest, in July 1944.

Hitler was a monster but, like many monsters, he could be very charming. He was a vegetarian who didn't drink and he loved to spend time at his mountain retreat in Berchtesgarden in southern Germany, where he kept his mistress **Eva Braun**, a shop assistant from Munich. He married Eva when Allied troops were storming into Berlin on 29 April 1945. Next day he probably shot himself. Eva took poison. As he'd previously ordered, their bodies were burned.

Holocaust *see* **Final Solution**

Home Guard
last ditch defenders

On 14 May 1940, as German forces were smashing their way south through Holland, the British government called for men between the ages of seventeen and sixty-five to join a 'Defence Force'. They were to sign up at their local police station. The police were overwhelmed - within twenty-four hours, a quarter of a million men joined what was soon to become known as the Home Guard. Many of them were veterans from World War I.

To start with, the men brought their own weapons, often shotguns or old World War I rifles which had been gathering dust in the attic. Some had no guns and a few even came with swords. There was no uniform to start with either. Gradually they became more organised. Ranks, as in the regular army, were introduced in February 1941.

The Home Guard, 'Dad's Army' as it's become known, never got the chance to fight the Germans. A good thing because they would have been flattened. The nearest they got to the enemy was when they arrested shot-down German airmen. But they did do useful work. They kept watch along the coasts and around airfields and factories, thus releasing regular soldiers for training.

Later in the war, the government used the Home Guard as training for youths before they were called up to join the regular army. By the summer of 1943, there were 1,750,000 Home Guard members and the average age was under thirty - so it wasn't so much a 'Dad's Army' after all.

ITMA
(It's That Man Again)
radio show which raised a laugh

ITMA, *'It's That Man Again'*, was a massively popular wartime radio comedy show. The 'Man' in question was meant to be **Hitler** whose ranting speeches were heard in Britain in 1939, when the show started.

The inventor and chief performer was Tommy Handley, mayor of 'Foaming-at-the-Mouth', an imaginary seaside resort. Handley invented a 'corporation cleaner', called Mrs Mopp, for Foaming-in-the-Mouth. There was also an 'Office of Twerps' which was a spoof on wartime government officials. He even invented a German spy, 'Herr Funf'. Millions tuned in to ITMA. They needed all the light relief they could get during the drab days of the war. The programme finished when Handley died in 1949.

⚔ Iwo Jima
island and battle
1945

The island of Iwo Jima lies about 1,000 kilometres (650 miles) south east of Tokyo. The name means 'Sulphur Island'. It has an extinct volcano on its southern tip and the whole place stinks of sulphur. 60,000 USA marines landed there in late February 1945. 22,000 Japanese defenders were waiting for them, dug into a network of caves and bunkers. The Japanese were so well dug in that American bombing and shells from warships before the main attack had hardly hurt them.

The fighting was very fierce and went on for nearly a month. One hill was so hard to capture that the Americans called it 'The Meat Grinder'. By the time the marines had won, nearly all the Japanese defenders were dead and so were 6,800 marines. From then on Iwo Jima was used as a base to launch bombing raids on Tokyo.

Joyce, William 'Lord Haw Haw'
he broadcast to Britain
1906-46

William Joyce was a leading Irish-American fascist who fled to Germany in 1939 to escape internment* in England. Once in Germany he became the English-language mouthpiece of the Nazis, broadcasting on radio. The nickname 'Lord Haw Haw' was first given to another English-language Nazi broadcaster. Joyce inherited it because he too broadcast in a phoney upper class accent (try laughing in an upper class way - haw, haw, haw). He made his last broadcast blind drunk from the ruins of Berlin and was executed for treason by the British authorities the following year.

kamikaze pilots
they behaved suicidally

On 19 October 1944, Vice Admiral Onishi Takajino of the Imperial Japanese Navy called for a force of suicide bombers to attack American aircraft carriers in the Philippines. Young, patriotic Japanese pilots were keen to volunteer. Their tactic was simple: to fly straight at an enemy ship and crash into it. (Ships were their main target.) Before the war ended, 5,000 young men had killed themselves in suicide attacks, destroying thirty-four ships and damaging hundreds of others. The best, if not the only, defence against the 'kamikazes' was to fill the sky with lead from concentrated anti-aircraft fire.

The name 'kamikaze' means 'divine wind'. It harks back to a typhoon which scattered a Mongol invasion fleet heading for Japan in 1281 AD.

♀ Land Army girls
they farmed for freedom

Once the war started, most young farm labourers joined the army. The few old men who were left couldn't keep up. The Land Army was an emergency organisation of women workers set up to replace the young men who had left. Land Girls might be sent anywhere in the country and they had to go. Their uniform was a green jumper, brown trousers, a brown 'slouch' hat and a khaki overcoat.

Haymaking, ploughing, mucking out - it was hard work and they only got seven days leave per year, compared to twenty-eight days in the army. Some town girls found it too hard, but others loved it, especially since they got the chance to work with animals. And some of them were hard enough themselves. One thousand of the Land Girls became rat catchers - perhaps they should have been in the real army.

lend lease
dollar-free deliveries - for a while

By the end of 1940, Britain was broke. The cost of fighting single-handed against Germany had been just too much. When the British asked for help, the Americans couldn't believe that the vast British Empire had simply run out of money. But then, American factories and cities weren't being bombed and the Americans weren't having to put their entire country on a war footing.

99 Finally, in December 1940, President **Roosevelt** at last realised that the British were telling the truth. On 11

March 1941, Congress passed a bill giving Roosevelt the power to supply America's allies with what they needed without asking for cash payments first. Under the 'Lend Lease' scheme, arms and other supplies flooded into Britain. The pay off came later, when the Americans demanded the right to sell their goods freely into the British and French Empires - which was a reasonable thing to ask for anyway.

Lend Lease was a generous programme and vital for the defeat of the Nazis. Britain received over half of all supplies and Russia got about 20%. The cut-off, by 112 President **Truman** immediately after Japan surrendered, was less generous. It left Britain with a war-shattered economy and nothing to pay for rebuilding. Several years passed before the Americans softened, with another scheme called Marshall Aid, to help war-damaged Europe - and Britain.

Leningrad, Siege of
872 days of hell
1941-44

On 22 June 1941, German armies flooded into Russia. 22 **Operation Barbarossa** had begun. They swept 28 forward using their usual *blitzkrieg* tactics and the Russians fell back before them. In the old Russian capital of Leningrad (now known by its original name, St. Petersburg) the citizens worked round the clock to build anti-tank defences, helped by 200,000 Red Army soldiers. When German troops reached the outskirts of Leningrad in July, the Russians were ready for them. The Germans tightened a noose round the city, which was almost totally cut off, but they didn't take it.

The siege went on for 872 days, nearly two and a half years. Some supplies got through by boat across Lake Ladoga and in winter by sled, and vegetables were grown on every spare strip of land within the city. But more than a million civilians died, of starvation, disease, wounds and cold. It was the most terrible battle of World War II.

Meanwhile, Russian armies were regrouping far to the east. They forced the Germans back from Moscow and finally, in January 1944, the siege of Leningrad was lifted. In 1965, the then Soviet government named Leningrad a 'Hero City', which indeed it was.

MacArthur, General Douglas
he hopped to victory

1880-1964

Douglas MacArthur was vain and self-important and hated criticism. He was also charming and a brilliant soldier. He commanded Allied forces in the Pacific region from 1942.

First he took Papua New Guinea from the Japanese. Then followed the re-conquest of the Phillipines, which was extremely bloody. It would have been even more bloody if it hadn't been for MacArthur's famous 'island hopping' strategy - he bypassed islands which were most strongly defended by the Japanese and picked off the weaker ones first.

CAN'T WE STOP OFF THERE, GENERAL?

NO WAY, SAILOR, THAT ISLAND'S WELL DEFENDED!

It was MacArthur who accepted the Japanese surrender on board the *Missouri* in September 1945. After that, the American government gave him the power to rule post-war Japan almost as if he was a new Japanese emperor. He ruled wisely, giving Japan a democratic constitution but leaving the real Emperor, **Hirohito**, still in place.

67

Maginot Line
futile French defence

Most of World War I took place on French soil. The French were determined: a) That Germany would never invade France again. b) That French troops would never suffer the horrors of trench* warfare again.

The Maginot Line, named after André Maginot the minister who dreamed it up, was a defensive line which the French built all along the German/French border, from Switzerland in the south east to Belgium in the north west. A long chain of heavy guns were mounted in forts with massive concrete walls. There were railway lines to bring up supplies and conditions for the defending troops were comfortable. Some forts even had air conditioning.

Unfortunately once World War II started, the whole Maginot Line turned out to be a complete waste of time and effort. The Germans attacked through Belgium and swung round the side of the Line. French troops manning it held out bravely, but France was soon conquered.

Montgomery, Bernard Law
Viscount Montgomery of Alamein 'Monty'

1887-1976

Montgomery was one of the most infuriating men who have ever lived. He was skinny, sharp-faced and incredibly pleased with himself - which was possibly understandable seeing as he was also a brilliant soldier. He had fought in World War I and in the British Expeditionary Force in 1939-40. In August 1942, **Churchill** gave him command of the Eighth Army in North Africa. The eighth had been badly bruised by the Germans under **Rommel**, but Montgomery breathed new fire into it. Soon (24 October - 4 November), he won a great victory at the second battle of **El Alamein**, the first major British victory of the war. Later he commanded Allied forces in the **D-Day** invasion of Europe, where he was so pig-headed that he drove **Eisenhower**, the American Supreme Commander, to distraction.

Montgomery had been wounded in World War I. The waste of life during that war always haunted him and he was determined not to waste the lives of his men in the same way. This made him a very cautious general. Too cautious some would say - but at least it was a fault in the right direction.

Munich Crisis
peace- but not for long
1938

In March 1938, **Hitler** gobbled up Austria. In May he began to threaten **Czechoslovakia**. He wanted to take over the **Sudetenland**, a German-speaking border area. He laid plans for an invasion of Czechoslovakia in September.

33 British Prime Minister **Chamberlain** flew over to talk him out of it, but Hitler took no notice and kept up the pressure, making one nasty speech after another. On 29 September 1938, the leaders of Italy, Britain and France met with Hitler in Munich to try to calm things down. Instead, they agreed that Germany could take over the Sudetenland after all. Next morning Hitler and Chamberlain signed an agreement to consult with each other rather than arguing. The crisis was over - because Hitler had got what he wanted. Chamberlain returned to Britain claiming he'd won 'peace with honour'. He hadn't, but perhaps he'd won some precious time to prepare for war.

Mussolini, Benito 'Il Duce'
he founded fascism
1883-1945

Benito Mussolini invented Fascism. In 1919, he founded a force of *fasci di combattimento* - fighting bands who would purify Italian society and lead Italy to greatness. His black-shirted fighters would be bound as tightly as the bands (*fasci*) of the ancient Roman lictors. Together they would found a new Roman Empire.

In 1922 Mussolini became Italy's youngest ever Prime Minister. He crushed all opposition, invaded Ethiopa (1935) and in June 1940 joined Word War II on the side of the Nazis. During the war the Italians lost almost every battle they fought in. They ended up being bullied by the Germans. Mussolini was forced from power by Italian opponents in 1943. Freed from his hotel-prison by German paratroopers he was taken to Munich and then given north Italy to rule as a German puppet dictator. In 1945 when Allied troops swept north, Mussolini tried to escape over the Alps disguised as a German soldier. He was recognised by Italian anti-fascists and he and his mistress were shot. Their bodies were hung upside down in central Milan in front of a cheering crowd.

Nagasaki *see* Hiroshima

Nazi Party
men of the master-race

The *Nationalsozialistische deutsche Arbeiterpartei* - National Socialist German Workers' Party - 'Nazi Party' for short - was founded in 1919 and soon copied the less pleasant features of **Benito Mussolini's** Italian Fascist Party. **Adolf Hitler** became its leader. The Nazis took power in Germany

83
70

in 1933 and crushed all opposition. Germans learned to obey their new leader (*Führer*) unquestioningly.

The Nazis were racists. They believed that the races of the world are locked in a never-ending struggle for land and power and that the German 'master race' would win the struggle. Defeated races would serve the master race and the Jews would be driven out of a racially purified Germany. The Germans would then rule for a thousand years, the 'Thousand Year *Reich*' (Empire).

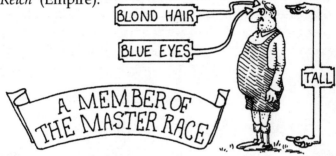

Nazi-Soviet Pact *see* **Russo-German Pact**

Nuremberg trials
tribunal for war criminals
1945-46

10 When World War II ended, the **Allies** let most ordinary Nazis go back to their homes, but they held onto the worst of them. The crimes of the Nazis were so horrific that some sort of justice had to be done. Twenty-four top Nazis were ordered to stand trial before an International Military Tribunal.

The Tribunal was held in the ancient German city of Nuremberg under a British judge, Lord Justice

Lawrence. Of the twenty-four accused, one of them committed suicide, one was acquitted and another was judged too ill and mad to stand trial. So twenty-one were tried and sentenced. Of these, seven got hefty prison terms, twelve were hanged, and one, 63 **Goering**, killed himself before he could be hanged. The twenty-first defendant Martin Bormann was thought to have escaped to South America and was tried in his absence. He was sentenced to death but was probably dead already. He'd probably died during the fall of Berlin in late April 1945.

Operation Overlord *see* **D-Day**

Operation Sealion *see* **Battle of Britain**

⚔ Pacific War
enormous eastern conflict

On 7 December 1941, the Japanese bombed the 90 American naval base of **Pearl Harbor** in Hawaii catching the Americans completely by surprise. Seventy American warships in the harbour were sunk or badly damaged. America declared war on Japan the next day. Within the next few months, Japanese forces took Hong Kong (on Christmas Day), 101 they stormed into Malaya, and then took **Singapore** (15 February 1943), Java, Burma and Borneo. On 6 May 1943, the last American troops left the

Philippines under their commander General
79 **MacArthur**. Pretty well the whole Far East was now under Japanese
rule.

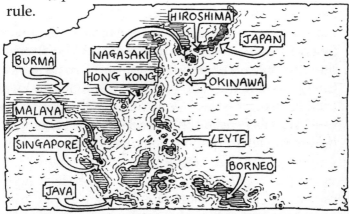

10 The **Allies** were reeling, but gradually, led by the Americans but with mainly Australian and New Zealand troops to start with, they began to fight back. It was a long and bloody war. The Americans 'island hopped' - they bypassed the strongest Japanese bases and took the weak ones, mopping up the stronger ones later. And the Japanese defended
75 their territory every step of the way. Their **kamikaze** pilots bombed American ships and their land soldiers fought to the last man.

The largest sea battle ever fought was won by the Americans at Leyte in the Philippines in October 1944. In June 1945 the Americans finally took **Okinawa** off the south coast of Japan after another horrendous fight. Okinawa was to be their base for the invasion of Japan itself. As it turned out, soldiers of both sides were spared what would have been a dreadful struggle - after the Americans dropped
68 nuclear bombs on **Hiroshima** and Nagasaki.

panzers 🔫

all tanked up

Tanks were first used in World War I but at that time most military thinkers saw them as just a back-up for foot soldiers. In the years before World War II, other military thinkers, among them a German officer called Heinz Guderian, began to see that armoured tank divisions on their own could attack much more quickly than infantry. 'Panzer' is German for 'armour'. When the war started, it was General Guderian's panzer divisions which stormed to victory, using *blitzkrieg* tactics - tanks backed up by dive bombers, with motorized infantry to mop up.

28

partisans ✠

they fought for freedom

10
19
While the main armies of the **Allies** and the **Axis Powers** slugged it out on the battlefields of Europe and Asia, brave men and women who were not members of any regular army fought to end German domination of their countries. In Yugoslavia, Poland and southern France partisans were a real nuisance to the German occupiers. German soldiers who

should have been off fighting the Allied armies had to stay behind to deal with the partisans - if they could find them.

🍄 Patton, George
'Old Blood-and-Guts'
cowboy in command
1885-1945

George Patton wore shiny boots and had a pair of ivory handled revolvers which he strapped to his thighs like an old time cowboy. He swore like a trooper and was generally very tough. He commanded the US 3rd Army during Operation Overlord and was the best US general of World War II. In less than a year he swept through France and into Germany, driving the Germans back before him. After a brilliant side-swipe northwards to help the Allied forces in the **Ardennes**, he drove on into Germany itself capturing huge numbers of German soldiers.

14

Patton was called 'Old Blood-and-Guts' by his men because he was so tough and fearless - too tough sometimes. He once struck a soldier who was in hospital with shell shock*. Patton died after a car crash.

⚓ Pearl Harbor 🚢
savage surprise attack
7 December 1941

Wai Momi is a large natural harbour on the south coast of Oahu Island, Hawaii, in the middle of the vast Pacific Ocean. The Hawaiians called it *Wai Momi*, meaning 'Pearl Waters' because of all the pearl oysters which they gathered from beneath its waters. In 1908 the USA built a naval station there, and by the 1940s 'Pearl Harbor' had become the USA's major naval base in the Pacific.

At 7.55 am on Sunday 7 December 1941, the peaceful skies above the harbour were shattered by the thunder of nearly two hundred Japanese dive bombers and other warplanes. They'd been launched from aircraft carriers which had steamed secretly to within air striking distance. Seventy unsuspecting American warships were berthed in the harbour at the time. It being Sunday many of their crews were ashore and there was almost no defence. By the time the Japanese left at 9.45 am, the American fleet was totally destroyed along with 180 aircraft on nearby airfields.

The Japanese hoped that this surprise attack (launched before war was declared between Japan and the USA) would give them a huge advantage. It had the opposite effect. The disaster of Pearl Harbor was what decided America to enter World War II on the side of the **Allies**.

Phoney War
the calm before the storm
1939-1940

On 3 September 1939, Britain and France declared war on Germany in support of **Poland** which had been invaded by the Germans. They then did almost nothing to actually help the poor Poles. British and French politicians feared that if they attacked German targets, Germany might retaliate - well, not all politicians actually, as **Winston Churchill** put it:

... the idea of not irritating the enemy did not commend itself to me.

The Germans for their part were only too pleased not to have to fight in two places at once. Until 9 April when the Germans invaded Norway, there was no fighting in the west. This period was dubbed the 'Phoney War' by an American newspaper. It was also called the 'Bore War' in Britain.

pill boxes
but not for medicine

A German tank trundles down a peaceful English lane. Nazi storm troopers leap out, they kick open the door of a pub that stands on the corner and gun down everyone inside.

It could have happened.

After the Allied retreat from **Dunkirk**, nothing stood between Britain and German invasion except the English channel and the **RAF**. If the RAF had lost the **Battle of Britain**, the Germans would move. The British government got ready. Pillboxes were concrete or brick gun positions. They were built at spots where they could hold up advancing German forces, for instance near important bridges. Other defensive measures were taken as well, such as planting long poles in fields near the coasts so that German gliders couldn't land in them.

Poland, invasion of
the spark that started the war
1939

By the end of March 1939, the Germans had finished their takeover of **Czechoslovakia**. But **Hitler** wanted still more *lebensraum* (living space) for the Germans. Poland was next on his list.

33 To warn Hitler off, **Neville Chamberlain** declared
that Britain would guarantee Polish independence
(31 March 1939). Hitler was furious. How dare the
British poke their noses into his business? He signed
107 a secret deal with the Russian dictator **Joseph Stalin**
(28 August), in which the two dictators agreed to
carve up Poland between them. On the morning of 1
September 1939, German troops stormed into
Poland. The Poles fought back like heroes but they
were totally outnumbered and outgunned. Britain
and France declared war on Germany two days later.

propaganda
the information war

All sides used propaganda during the war. They used it to keep their own people cheerful and to make the other side feel gloomy and to make them want to give up. Both sides also used censorship so that their press and radio didn't give away secrets which would be helpful to the enemy. In Britain, letters home from members of the armed forces were checked. The office of censorship in Liverpool would glance through the letters and often they would brush an X across a page to test for secret messages written in invisible ink.

'White' propaganda meant telling the truth to the enemy - at least, the bits that you wanted him or her to know about. In the long run it was probably more effective than 'black' propaganda which meant telling lies. There were lots of ways to do black propaganda. Leaflets were dropped from planes or fired from artillery shells. Pamphlets were forged to look as if they'd been printed by the enemy, but with false information. 'Whispering campaigns' started false rumours doing the rounds.

Radio broadcasts were the most effective form of propaganda - black and white. The Germans used 75 **Lord Haw Haw** to broadcast black propaganda in English, never realising that the British thought he was funny. White radio was used by all the leaders to encourage 70 their people. **Hitler** broadcast his ranting 35 speeches, **Churchill's** speeches are still fondly remembered and President 99 **Roosevelt** specialised in his 'fireside chats'.

Quisling, Vidkun
1887-1945

Vidkun Quisling was a home-grown, Norwegian fascist who ruled German-occupied Norway for the Germans from 1942-1945. He was executed as a traitor when the war ended and his name has become another word for a leader who works for the enemy.

⊘ rationing
sharing out shortages

Britain is a small island with a lot of people living on it. In 1939, 60% of all food eaten in Britain came from abroad. Once war started and German **U-boats** set to work on British merchant ships, it became impossible to carry on bringing in such large quantities of food. And what imported food there was tended to be pretty horrible. Powdered egg and powdered milk are not the stuff of classy cooking, to put it mildly.

The British had to grow more of their own food so as not to starve. They had to 'dig for victory'. Every available scrap of land was dug and used for planting vegetables, even roadside verges. By 1943, there

113

were 3.5 million allotments. Many people joined 'pig clubs'. They clubbed together to buy a pig and then fed it on their kitchen waste. When it was slaughtered they shared out the bits.

But despite all these efforts, there was still a shortage of food compared to before the war. The government began to ration food in January 1940, because, if they hadn't, better-off families would have scoffed what little there was. The first things to be rationed were butter, sugar and bacon/ham. Other foods soon followed as well as petrol, clothing and textiles. Soap was included in 1942 - wartime Britain was a smellier place than it is today.

Rationing worked on a points system. Everyone had a ration book. The coupons in the book were worth so many points each, and different food rations needed different numbers of points. Adults got sixteen points per week, and they could save them up if they wanted to.

ARE YOU SURE HE'S MEANT TO LIVE IN THE KITCHEN?

reprisals
simply, murder

The Germans used reprisal killings as a way of crushing resistance to their rule in the lands that they conquered. If one German soldier was shot by the resistance movement, they might shoot ten innocent

villagers in reprisal. That way they hoped to make
the resistance unpopular with the locals.

⚜ resistance
(see also partisans)
behind enemy lines

The Nazis ruled occupied Europe
with an iron fist, but in all the
countries that they occupied,
there was resistance to their
rule. Resistance movements
gathered information about
German troop movements to
send to the Allied forces,
they bombed railway lines
and sabotaged factories,
and if they were strong
enough they attacked German
118 soldiers. **Women** came into their
own in the resistance movements.
They often carried messages
because they were less likely to be
stopped, and some became
organisers and leaders.

Passive resistance was almost as bad for the Germans
as active resistance. Passive resistance meant
resistance without doing anything: anything from

refusing to speak to the Germans or misdirecting them if they asked you the way, through to strikes or go-slows in the factories. The French railway system was almost useless to the Germans because French railwaymen made sure it was just that - useless. Somehow trains never ran on time and they were always breaking down.

Rommel, Erwin
 'Desert Fox'
fast-moving German general
1891-1944

Erwin Rommel was a brilliant German general who used surprise and fast tank movements to defeat his enemies. He led Germany's Afrika Corps in North Africa, where he drove the British out of Tunisia and all the way to the border with Egypt. There he was defeated by **Montgomery** at the Second Battle of **El Alamein** (October/November 1942). Montgomery then drove him all the way back to Tunisia again. By that time Rommel was ill. He was sent back to Germany to get better.

81
51

70 In May 1943, **Hitler** put him in charge of German defences against the expected Allied invasion from Britain. Rommel ringed the west coast of Europe with concrete gun forts, underwater obstacles, tank traps and

'Rommel's asparagus' - poles set up in fields to get in
43 the way of Allied glider landings. After the **D-Day**
landings he was wounded in the head during an air
attack on his car. Soon after that he was accused of
109 being part of the **von Stauffenberg** July bomb plot
against Hitler. Hitler allowed him to take poison
rather than be executed.

Roosevelt, Franklin Delano
partially paralysed president
1882-1945

In August 1921, Franklin Roosevelt caught polio and
was completely paralysed for a while. He never fully
recovered the use of his legs. From that time on he
spent most of his waking hours in a wheelchair. It
was from a wheelchair that he became President of
America four times, and from a wheelchair that he
led America into World War II.

To start with, Roosevelt tried to keep America out of
the war. Later he saw that the Nazis were truly evil.
35 **Churchill**, whose mother was an American, helped
to persuade him. In March 1941, Roosevelt started
77 **Lend Lease**, supplying arms and other supplies
without cash payments, first to Britain and then to
other enemies of Germany. After the Japanese attack
90 on **Pearl Harbor** in December 1941, America was
ready for war and Roosevelt was more than ready to
lead the war effort. From then on he was central to
the Allied campaign. He died of a heart attack in
70 early April 1945, just weeks before **Hitler** committed
suicide and the Germans surrendered.

Royal Air Force
in clouds of glory

In 1939, when the war started, the RAF had just 1,911 planes ready to fight with 193,000 men to man them in the air and on the ground. The *Luftwaffe* had 3,609 planes and more than half a million men. The Battle of Britain was not an equal battle. In early September 1940, the Germans were shooting down British planes faster than the British could build new ones to replace them. However, after that the RAF grew stronger and stronger. By the time the war ended in 1945, there were over a million men and women in the Force and thousands of planes.

Royal Navy
they helped turn the tide

Compared to the **RAF**, which was just twenty-one years old, the Royal Navy was a grizzled old age pensioner. It was four hundred years old and its 180,000 sailors and marines had a vital role to play in protecting supply convoys to Russia and from America, and in keeping up a blockade of Germany itself. By the end of the war there were over 800,000 men and women in the service.

Russo-German Pact
(Nazi-Soviet Pact)
friendship between enemies
1939-41

Nazis hated communists* and communists hated Nazis. That was just how it was. What more shocking than when, on 23 August 1939, **Hitler**, the Nazi leader of Germany, and **Stalin**, the communist leader of the USSR*, signed a 'Treaty of Non-Aggression' with each other and rounded this off with a 'Treaty of Friendship' that September? Of course, Hitler and Stalin only meant non-aggression against each other so that they could be even more aggressive towards everyone else. The real secret reason for the treaties was to carve up **Poland**. When Hitler invaded Poland in September 1939, the USSR* grabbed its share of the east of the country.

The Russo-German pact lasted until Hitler invaded the USSR in **Operation Barbarossa**, which began on 22 June 1941.

⚔ Singapore, fall of
feeble British surrender
1942

The island of Singapore, just off the Malayan coast, is a very rich and tidy place nowadays. In 1942, it was a place of fear and crowded with refugees. The

Japanese pushed the British out of Malaysia during 1941 and by early 1942, British troops had retreated onto the island, which was then a major British naval base. Japanese forces landed on a moonlit night on 8-9 February. British resistance was feeble. By 15 February, it was all over. The British commander, General Percival, surrendered. The Japanese took 62,000 British and British Indian forces prisoner.

SOE
(Special Operations Executive)
So, you're an agent are you?

The SOE was set up in the summer of 1940. Its headquarters were in Baker Street, London, near the rooms of legendary detective Sherlock Holmes. Its

job was to train secret agents and to place them inside German-occupied Europe.

The agents, both men and women, were first taught the tricks of their trade: how to carry messages in rolled up cigarettes and smoke them if discovered, how to take suicide pills if caught, how to work a short wave radio, how to plant explosives and sometimes how to fight with their bare hands.

Usually they were dropped into enemy territory by parachute. The SOE had a special plane, the Lysander. It could fly long distances without refuelling and could land in a field just 32 metres long. Once landed, usually at night, the agent was on his or her own until the local **resistance** found him or her. To be successful they had to be totally fluent in the local language. If caught, they were usually tortured for their information then shot as **spies**. Many very brave men and women died in this way.

Speer, Albrecht
architect of an evil empire
1905-81

70 Albrecht Speer started off as a Nazi architect. **Hitler**
    used him to design overblown building projects for
111 his **'Thousand Year'** empire. Then in 1942, Hitler
    made him minister for armaments. Using slave
40 labour, much of it from the **concentration camps**,
    Speer tripled German arms production. After the war
85 was over, he was tried at the **Nuremberg Trials** and
    spent the next twenty years in prison in Berlin.

 spies
they searched for secrets

Spies work for the enemy but pretend not to - unlike
soldiers who wear the uniform of their country and
don't pretend to be anything other than what they
are. If spies are caught they're often executed.

Sixteen enemy spies
were executed in
Britain during the
war. The Germans
sent in about twenty
per year, either
dropped by
parachute or landed
from submarines but
the British SIS (Secret

Intelligence Service, now MI6) was very good at spotting them. Not a single German spy managed to do any serious spying on British soil. The reason that only sixteen were executed was because, when caught, most of them were 'turned' - they were persuaded to work for Britain. They were then fed false information to pass on to their masters back in Germany.

The Germans had two spy networks. One was run by the SS and the other was the *Abwehr*. Many *Abwehr* agents were anti-Nazi. Being a secret service they got to see secret information about the concentration camps and other Nazi horrors, so they understood what the Nazis were really like. Several *Abwehr* agents were involved in plots against **Hitler**. Finally the *Abwehr* itself was destroyed by its SS rivals.

🚫 spivs
crooked customers

'Spiv' was slang for the flashy, small-time crooks who operated the black market. The spiv look included wide jacket collars, wide shoulder pads and fashionable trousers.

⚔ SS
(Schutzstaffeln)
men in black

70 The SS was formed in 1925 to be **Hitler's** bodyguard. It grew into the most feared force in Nazi Europe. On the orders of its leader

66 **Heinrich Himmler**, a fanatical Nazi, only perfect specimens of the Master Race could join it. It was said that a filling in your tooth was enough to keep you out. These blond, blue-eyed members of the Master Race in their smart, black uniforms felt superior, even to other Germans. SS members were trained to be racist and were utterly cruel to their enemies.

The dreaded Gestapo, secret police force, was part of the SS as were the *Totenkopfverbünde* (Deaths-Head Battalions), who ran the concentration camps.

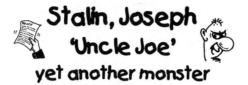

Stalin, Joseph
'Uncle Joe'
yet another monster

1879-1953

Stalin became ruler of the communist* USSR in the 1920s. He was utterly ruthless and in many ways he was more of a monster than **Hitler** himself. In the summer of 1939 the two monsters signed a non-aggression pact (the **Russo-German Pact**). The pact meant that they agreed not to attack each other - which meant that Hitler was free to invade Poland and thus start World War II. Meanwhile, Stalin grabbed chunks of eastern Poland and other lands in eastern Europe. Then in **Operation Barbarossa** (June 1941) the Germans invaded Russia. Stalin was deeply shocked but he came out of shock a few days later, ready to lead Soviet resistance to the Germans.

Stalin believed that people work best when frightened, so he made sure that his own people were almost as frightened of him as they were of the Nazis. One of his best generals had stainless steel teeth because his teeth had been kicked out by Stalin's secret police. Stalin also issued Order No. 270 which stated that any Soviet soldier taken prisoner by the Germans was a traitor - they would have to fight to the death or be shot by their own side.

After the Germans invaded Russia, Britain and Russia found themselves on the same side. British newspapers began to portray Stalin as kindly 'Uncle Joe'. At the Yalta Conference between Stalin, **Churchill** and **Roosevelt** in 1945, when the leaders discussed what to do after they had won the war, Uncle Joe suggested that they kill between 50-100,000 German officers straight away. Churchill felt sick and Roosevelt thought Stalin was joking. He wasn't.

35
99

✗ Stalingrad, Battle of
when the Germans met their match
1942-3

Stalingrad, now called Volgograd, straddles the mighty River Volga in the centre of Russia. It was the furthest east the Germans ever got. They smashed their way into it on 12 September 1942.

107 **Stalin** couldn't bear to lose a city which had his name on it. He decided to defend Stalingrad whatever the cost. Although the Germans fought their way from house to house and street to street as far as the city centre, they never managed to shift the Russians from other parts of the city. In November, fresh Soviet armies swept round the city to the west thus surrounding the German attackers. Now the tables 70 were turned. **Hitler** tried to keep his troops supplied by air but it was hopeless. On 31 January the German General Paulus surrendered. About 800,000 Germans and their allies died during the battle.

Stauffenberg, Count Berthold von
very brave German conspirator

1907-44

Count von Stauffenberg was a German officer. While recovering from the loss of his left eye and right hand during fighting in North Africa, he decided
70 that **Hitler** was a disaster who had to go. Stauffenberg joined a conspiracy of army officers which planned to kill the *Führer*. On 20 July 1944, he placed a bomb in a briefcase in Hitler's headquarters at Rastenberg in central Germany. He put it under a table near Hitler's chair. Unluckily another officer moved the briefcase and when the bomb went off Hitler was unharmed. Stauffenberg was executed that night.

Sudetenland, annexation of
a bothersome border

1938

The Sudetenland was a border region of
42 **Czechoslovakia**. About three million Germans lived there. It had only become part of Czechoslovakia following Germany's defeat in World War I.
70 Germany, and **Hitler** in particular, wanted it back.

In 1935 the Sudeten Germans voted for their local Nazi party in large numbers and in 1938, in the

82 **'Munich Agreement'**, the leaders of Britain, France and Italy agreed that they and their land must be returned to Germany. All of which gave Hitler a good excuse to gobble up the rest of Czechoslovakia a year later.

swastika
it depends how you look at it

The right-handed swastika symbol is still used in Indian culture, where it may have come from and is a symbol for the Sun. 'Swastika' means 'helps well-being' in Sanskrit, an ancient Indian language. In ancient Germany the left-handed swastika may have stood for the hammer of the god Thor and in ancient India it stood for the night, for Kali the goddess of destruction and for magic.

70 **Hitler** adopted the right-handed swastika as the
84 symbol of the **Nazi Party**. He thought it had a

German origin. He got the wrong one. The left-handed one would have been more appropriate in every way.

Third Reich
an empire too many

The First *Reich* (means 'empire') was the Medieval Holy Roman Empire, based in Germany, the Second Reich was nineteenth century Germany as made into a powerful, unified country by Count Otto von Bismarck. The Third Reich was to be the Nazi *Reich*. It would last a thousand years and it would 70 dominate the world. That was **Hitler's** plan.

ALL MINE!

⚔ Tobruk, Seige of
the Allies' African toe-hold
1941

In the spring of 1941, German armies under General 98 **Rommel** swept east through North Africa on their way to British-held Egypt. They swept right past the Libyan port of Tobruk defended by just two Australian brigades. Rommel didn't like this enemy thorn in his flank. Over the coming months he tried several times to take the port but without success. During summer the Australians were taken off in British ships and replaced by British and Polish troops, but the siege went on - until the following June, when Tobruk eventually fell and 35,000 Allied troops were captured.

Tojo, General Hideki
top Japanese commander

1884-1948

General Tojo was Japanese Prime Minister for most of World War II. For a while he had almost total power since he was top general as well as top politician. If anyone was responsible for the terrible Japanese war crimes, it was him. After Japan surrendered on 2 September 1945, Tojo shot himself but was nursed back to health. He was then tried as a war criminal and hanged.

Truman, Harry S.
president who dropped a bombshell

1884-1972

Harry Truman was Vice-President of the USA when 99 **Roosevelt** died on 12 April 1945. He took over immediately, and became President. By then, the war in Europe was as good as over, but in the Far East the

Japanese were determined to fight to the last. On the island of Okinawa even the civilians fought to the death. The war might go on for months or even years and many more were bound to die.

Since 1940, American, British and refugee European scientists had been working on the top-secret Manhattan Project - to develop an atomic bomb. That bomb was now ready for use and Truman decided to use it. On 6 August 1945, 'Little Boy' was dropped on the Japanese city of **Hiroshima**, killing 70,000 immediately. Three days later, 'Fat Boy' was dropped on Nagasaki. Japan surrendered on 14 August.

U-boats
they packed a punch

U-Boat stands for *Unterseeboot*, German for 'submarine'. U-boat 'wolf packs' sank a vast number of Allied merchant ships during the Battle of the Atlantic.

For most of the war, all submarines, including U-boats, were designed to travel fast and far on the surface and only to submerge when they had to. A typical U-boat with a crew of forty-four men could travel up to 6,500 kilometres (4,036 miles) without refuelling, but underwater, it could only move at speed for a few hours. This was because their diesel engines wouldn't work underwater where there was no free oxygen for the diesel to burn in. They had to rely on rather feeble, battery-powered electric engines for underwater work. Another problem was that, if a U-boat stayed submerged for more than a day, the air inside became so foul that it was hard to breathe.

SPLUTTER! KOFF! KOFF! GASP!

In 1944, the Germans developed the *schnorchel* pipe. Air was taken down the pipe to the diesel engine. U-boats could now travel long distances just below the surface without coming up for air.

 ULTRA

British codeword for all information gathered from
52 **Enigma** signals and decoded by the brain boxes at
Bletchley Park.

VE Day
8 May 1945

VE Day stands for 'Victory in Europe Day'. It was
celebrated in all the Allied countries. Church bells
rang and vast, happy crowds gathered in the main
cities.

Vichy France
what the Germans left over

70 When **Hitler** invaded France on 10 May 1940, the
French government fled first to Bordeaux and then
to Vichy, which is a small resort town in central
France where tourists go to 'take the waters'. After it

became a centre of government, Vichy was still a good place to take a bath but not a good place to be a Free Frenchman in. The new French leader, Marshal Pétain (1856-1951), a World War I hero, quickly signed an armistice* with the conquerors. Germany would rule in the north west but Pétain's government would carry on in the south east with Vichy as its capital. Pétain set himself up in the Hôtel du Parc near the centre of town. In November 1942, the Germans took over the south east of France as well, and Pétain had to rule with the Germans literally looking over his shoulder.

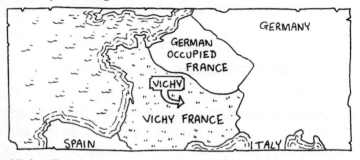

Vichy France was never accepted as the true French government by the Free French under de Gaulle. Although not Nazi, it carried out many Nazi policies. Vichy police rounded up Jews to be sent to death camps in Germany. Meanwhile, thousands of young men took to the hills
97 to join the **resistance** so as not to have to work for the Germans. Vichy police joined the Gestapo in trying to hunt them down. After the war was over, Pétain was tried and sentenced to
45 death as a traitor. **De Gaulle** let him off with life imprisonment.

⊘ VJ-Day 🏃

15 August 1945

The day after the Japanese High
Command agreed to surrender
unconditionally is remembered
as VJ-Day in Allied countries,
although some people say
VJ-Day is really on 2
September when the
Japanese actually signed
the surrender document.

Warsaw ghetto ✠
where the Jews fought back

From Medieval times, Jews had been forced to live in
a special Jewish quarter in many cities in north Africa
and then in Europe. The word ghetto was first used
to describe these Jewish quarters in Medieval Venice.
Ghettos were usually surrounded by walls to protect
the Jews from attack - and to keep them in.

The Nazis liked the idea of ghettos. They could use
them to imprison large numbers of Jews before they
killed them. One of the largest was the ghetto in
Warsaw, the Polish capital city. Jews from all the
surrounding area were herded into it, until by the
summer of 1943 500,000 were crammed into it in
appalling conditions.

At the same time, thousands were being shipped out
to extermination camps, so that by September
numbers were down again to around 55,000. It was

obvious that something unspeakably dreadful was going on. The following January the Jews at last began to fight back. They had few weapons but nothing to lose. They were determined fighters. They would shoot then disappear into the rabbit warren of hiding places in the ghetto before the Germans could retaliate. The unequal fight went on until 19 April 1943, when 3,000 crack German troops with tanks and all manner of guns forced their way in. And still the fight went on - until 8 May, when the Germans captured the Jewish headquarters. The Jewish leaders killed themselves rather than surrender. Others fought on into July.

♀ women
they fought too

Women with guns - shocking! The first country ever officially to ask women to fight in its armed forces was the USSR* in 1942. No other country in World War II went quite that far, but the war still brought massive changes for nearly all women on both sides. British women 'manned' **anti-aircraft** guns. This was revolutionary even though they weren't meant to pull the trigger. Lots of women fought and died in unofficial **resistance** movements all over Europe, and for the British **SOE**. Many more joined back-up or 'auxiliary' women's forces.

In 1941, Britain became the first country to conscript women. That meant that young women had to work where they were told to work - or to join the auxiliary services. By 1944, one in ten of all members of the British armed services were women. The women's services were known by their initials:

ATS - Auxiliary Territorial Service.
WAAFs - Women's Auxiliary Air Force. They did a lot of skilled maintentance work.
WRNS, or 'Wrens' - the Women's Royal Naval Service.

For those women who didn't join the auxiliary services, the choice was basically between the **Land Army**, armaments factories, nursing and civil defence (for instance, manning the barrage balloons). By 1943, nearly eight million women were in paid jobs. The government laid on special nurseries near factories so that women could keep an eye on their children. After the war was over, many of these women went back to being housewives and to looking after their children. It took another thirty years before very large numbers of women were back at work again.

Workers' Playtime
lunchtime radio

Workers' Playtime was a lunchtime radio programme broadcast into factory canteens all over Britain three times a week. It was meant to cheer people up so that they would work hard for the war effort and it was very popular.

WVS
an army of helpers

The Women's Volunteer Service was started in 1938 by Lady Reading. Basically it was a million middle-aged women volunteers who worked like Trojans dishing out soup and other comforts to the victims of German bombing, and to returned and wounded soldiers and such like, throughout the war. The WVS was a vital part of the war effort.

Zhukov, General Georgi
 redoubtable Russian general
1896-1974

General Georgi Zhukov led the Russian forces which saved Moscow from capture by the Germans. He helped to free **Leningrad** from its siege, captured Warsaw and led the final attack on Berlin. It was General Zhukov who accepted the German surrender for the Russians.

78

GLOSSARY

ARMISTICE: agreement to stop fighting.

ATTRITION: in a war of attrition, the idea is to destroy as many men and weapons belonging to the other side as possible, even if you lose an equal number yourself. The side with the most men and weapons ends up winning - whatever the cost.

COMMUNISTS: communists believe that all 'means of production, distribution and exchange' (ie factories, shops and so on) should be owned and controlled by the people - which in practice usually means the government. *See below* SOVIET UNION.

INTERNMENT: in wartime, governments often lock up enemy nationals who just happen to be living in the opposing country when the war starts - even if they have committed no crimes.

SHELL SHOCK: the noise and the terror of being fired at can drive men crazy in a nervous disorder called shell shock. Symptoms include nightmares and extreme irritability.

SOVIET UNION: From 1922 through to the 1980s, Russia dominated a large group of neighbouring, communist-ruled countries. Together they were known as the 'Union of Soviet Socialist Republics' or USSR.

USSR *see above* SOVIET UNION.

INDEX

Abwehr 105

ack-acks *see* **anti-aircraft guns**

Adlertag see Eagle Day

air raid shelters 8-9,17

Allies, the 10,16,45,54,67, 85,87,88,91

Anderson, Dr David 8

Anderson shelters 8

***Anschluss* 10-11**

anti-aircraft guns 11-12,118

Anzio, Battle of 13

appeasement 34

Ardennes, Battle of 14-15, 89

Arnhem, Battle of 15-16

ARP wardens 17,27,37

Atlantic, Battle of 17-19

ATS 119

Auxiliary Territorial Service *see* ATS

Axis Powers 19-20,88

Baedeker raids 20-21

Balloon Command 24

Barbarossa, Operation 22-23,29,78,107

barrage balloons 11,23-24, 119

Battle of Britain Day 32

Battle of the Bulge *see* **Ardennes, Battle of**

Beer Hall Putsch 63,70

***Bismarck* 24**

Bismarck, Otto von 111

black market 25-26

blackout 17,26-27

Blitz 8,17,27-28,32,35,37, 56,57,64

***blitzkrieg* 28-29**,78,88

Bomba 53

Bomber Command 21,64

Bomber Harris *see* **Harris, Arthur**

Bormann, Martin 86

Braun, Eva 29-30,63,71

Britain, Battle of 30-32,48, 63,92,100

Burma-Thailand Railway 32-33

Chamberlain, Neville 33-34,35,42,83,93

Churchill, Winston 34, 35-36,46,50,82,91,94,99, 108

Civil Defence 37-38,119

clothes 38-39

collaborators 39-40

Cologne 65

Colossus 53

concentration camps 40-41,58,63,67,105,106

convoys 18,100

Czechoslovakia, invasion of 42,82,92,110

Dad's Army *see* **Home Guard**
Dambusters 42-43
D-Day 43-45,51,59,61, 82,99
De Gaulle, Charles 45-46, 116
dig for victory 95
Dönitz, Karl 19
Doodle-bugs *see* **flying bombs**
Dorsetshire 25
Dowding, Hugh 30,31, **47-48**
Dresden 48-49,65
Dunkirk 30,47,**49-50**,54,92

Eagle Day 31
Eichmann, Adolf 58
Eisenhower, Dwight 44,**51**, 82
El Alamein 51-52,82,98
Enigma machine 52-54,115
ENSA 54
Entertainments National Service Association *see* **ENSA**
evacuation 55-57

fascists 39,75,83,95
Fighter Command 30,32,47
Final Solution 40,**57-59**,63, 66,67
flying bombs 24,57,**59-60**
Free French 46,51,116

gas masks 60-61

Gestapo 63,66,106,116
GI brides 61-62
GIs 61-62
Goebbels, Joseph 62-63
Goering, Hermann 31,32, **63-64**,86
Guderian, Heinz 88

Handley, Tommy 73
Harris, Arthur 21,49,**64-65**
Heydrich, Reinhard 66
Himmler, Heinrich 66-67, 106
Hirohito 67-68,80
Hiroshima 68-69,87,113
Hitler, Adolf 11,14,17,29,30, 31,32,33,34,36,42,50,54, 57,59,62,63,66,67, **70-71**,73,82,83,84,92,93, 98,99,101,104,105,106, 107,109,110,111,115,
Holocaust 59
Home Guard 71-72
Hood 24
Hurricanes 30,32,47

ITMA 73
Iwo Jima 74

Joyce, William 75,94

kamikaze pilots 75-76,87
King George V 25
Kwai, Bridge over the River 33

Land Army girls 76-77,119

Lend Lease 77-78,99
Leningrad, Siege of
  78-79,121
Leyte, Battle of 87
Lord Haw Haw *see* Joyce,
  William
Lübeck 21,65
Lucas, Major-General 13
Luftwaffe 30,31,32,50,63,
  100

MacArthur, Douglas 68,
  79-80,87
Maginot, André 80
Maginot Line 80-81
Manhattan Project 113
Marshall Aid 78
Mein Kampf 70
Montgomery, Bernard Law
  16,52,81-82,98
Morrison, Herbert 9
Morrison shelters 9
Mulberry harbours 45
Munich Crisis (or,
  Agreement) 34,37,42,
  82-83,110
Mussolini, Benito 83-84

Nagasaki 69,87,113
Nazi Party 62,63,70,84-85,
  110
Nuremberg trials 64,
  85-86,104

Okinawa, Battle of 87,113
Onishi Takajino 75
Overlord, Operation 44,89

Pacific War 86-87
panzers 14,16,52,88
partisans 22,88-89
Patton, George 15,89
Pearl Harbor 10,18,86,
  90-91,99
Percival, Arthur 102
Pétain, Henri 45,116
Phoney War 17,56,91
pig clubs 96
pill boxes 92
Poland, invasion of 91,
  92-93,107
Prince of Wales 24
propaganda 93-94

Quisling, Vidkun 95

radar 31,38,47
RAF 30,31,32,43,45,50,92,
  100
rationing 25,26,95-96
Reading, Lady 120
reprisals 96-97
resistance 44,97-98,116,
  118
Rodney 25
Rommel, Erwin 52,82,
  98-99,111
Roosevelt, Franklin 36,46,
  77,94,99,108,112
Royal Air Force *see* RAF
Royal Navy 18,24,25,100
Rundstedt, Karl von 50
Russo-German Pact 101,
  107

saturation bombing 21,65
Scharnhorst 24
Schicklgruber, Adolf *see*
 Hitler, Adolf
Sealion, Operation 30,31,32
Secret Intelligence Service
 see SIS
Singapore, fall of 101-2
SIS 104-5
SOE 66,**102-3**,119
Special Operations
 Executive *see* **SOE**
Speer, Albrecht 104
spies 103,**104-5**
Spitfires 30,31
spivs 26,**106**
SS 40,66,105,**106**
Stalingrad, Battle of 108
Stalin, Joseph 23,93,101,
 107-8
**Stauffenberg, Berthold
 von** 71,99,**109**
**Sudetenland, annexation
 of** 34,42,82,83,**109-10**
swastika 110-1

Third Reich 85,104,**111**
thousand bomber raids 65
Thousand Year Reich *see*
 Third Reich
Tobruk, Siege of 111-12
Tojo, Hideki 112
Truman, Harry 78,**112-13**
Turing, Alan 53

U-boats 18,19,95,**113-14**
ULTRA 13,19,53,**115**

utility clothes 39

V-1 bomb 24,59
V-2 bomb 60
VE Day 115
Vichy France 40,**115-16**
VJ-Day 117

WAAFs 23,119
Wallis, Barnes 43
Warsaw ghetto 117-18
women 118-20
Women's Auxiliary Air Force
 see WAAFs
Women's Royal Naval
 Service *see* WRNS
Women's Volunteer Service
 see **WVS**
Workers' Playtime 120
WRNS 119
WVS 38,**120**

Yalta conference 108

Zhukov, Georgi 121

NOW READ ON

If you want to know more about World War II, see if your local library or bookshop has either of these books.

WHAT THEY DON'T TELL YOU ABOUT THE BLITZ
Also by Bob Fowke (Hodder Children's Books 2002). The bombing of London began on 24 August 1940 and carried on until May of the following year. This book tells the story of those terrible raids and of the brave men, women and children who fought to survive even while the bombs were falling.

WHAT THEY DON'T TELL YOU ABOUT WORLD WAR II
Also by Bob Fowke (Hodder Children's Books 2001). When gas-masked horses stood up to evil bombers and children played with live ammunition - and worse - the story of World War II as you've never heard it before!

ABOUT THE AUTHOR

Bob Fowke is a popular author of children's information books. Writing under various pen names and with various friends and colleagues, he has created many unusual and entertaining works on all manner of subjects.

There's always more to his books than meets the eye - look at all the entries in the index of this one!

Who? What? When?
ORDER FORM

0 340 85185 6	TUDORS	£4.99
0 340 85184 8	VICTORIANS	£4.99
0 340 85186 4	WORLD WAR I	£4.99
0 340 85187 2	WORLD WAR II	£4.99

All Hodder Children's books are available at your local bookshop or newsagent, or can be ordered direct from the publisher. Just write to the address below. Prices and availability subject to change without notice.

Hodder Children's Books, Cash Sales Department, Bookpoint, 130 Milton Park, Abingdon, Oxon, OX14 4SB, UK.
Email address: orders@bookpoint.co.uk

Please enclose a cheque or postal order made payable to Bookpoint Ltd to the value of the cover price and allow the following for postage and packing:
UK & BFPO - £1.00 for the first book, 50p for the second book, and 30p for each additional book ordered, up to a maximum charge of £3.00. OVERSEAS & EIRE - £2.00 for the first book, £1.00 for the second book, and 50p for each additional book.

If you have a credit card you may order by telephone - (01235) 400414 (lines open 9am-6pm, Monday to Saturday; 24 hour message answering service). Alternatively you can send a fax on 01235 400454.